MW00643304

Natalia Ilyin

CHASING THE PERFECT

Thoughts on Modernist Design in Our Time

METROPOLIS BOOKS

EDITOR Diana Murphy
PRODUCTION EDITOR Adrian Crabbs
DESIGNER Matthew Monk
PHOTO CONSULTANT Emily Speers Mears
PHOTO RESEARCHER Evelyn Dilworth
SEPARATIONS AND PRINTING Asia Pacific Offset, Inc., China

Set in Scala and Scala Sans, a pair of faces designed by Martin Majoor in 1991
Printed on Gold East Matt

FRONTISPIECE Albrecht Heubner, Minimal Dwelling, project, 1927

Library of Congress Cataloging-in-Publication Data

Ilyin, Natalia, 1957-
  Chasing the perfect : thoughts on modernist design in our time / Natalia Ilyin.– 1st ed.
    p. cm.
  ISBN 1-933045-21-3
  1. Ilyin, Natalia, 1957- 2. Commercial artists–United States–Biography. I. Title.
  NC999.4.I46 2005
  741.6'092–dc22

    2005021657

METROPOLIS BOOKS is a joint publishing program of:

D.A.P./Distributed Art Publishers, Inc.
155 Sixth Avenue, 2nd floor
New York NY 10013
TEL 212 627 1999   FAX 212 627 9484
www.artbook.com

Metropolis Magazine
61 West 23rd Street, 4th floor
New York NY 10010
TEL 212 627 9977   FAX 212 627 9988
www.metropolismag.com

Available through D.A.P./Distributed Art Publishers, Inc., New York

For my father, Boris Ilyin

CONTENTS

You are about to go on a personal journey with a brave designer. Throw aside your received wisdom about what it means to be modern, and let Natalia Ilyin show you what modernism has really done to us, each and every one of us. Meander with her as she reveals our obsession with perfection, and decide for yourself how this obsession has shaped your own life. If you are a designer, this book will help you think more deeply about your work. If you are a user of modern design—and who hasn't been to a mall, an airport, a school, an office, as well as used the myriad appliances and other objects that abound in consumer societies?—you need to read this book.

Although there's a lot of writing about design, those who explain design to practitioners and to the public rarely expose their own psyches. Natalia does this, to the point of personal pain. Humor, too, is largely missing from design writing. Natalia is funny. Plus, she has an uncanny ability to combine passionate argument with rational thought. Her writing style mirrors her hilarious, insightful, and always intellectually stimulating conversations. So if you don't have the good fortune to engage her in person, get to know her in these pages—it's worth your time.

SUSAN S. SZENASY

This dizziness in the face of *les espaces infinis*—only overcome if we dare to gaze into them without any protection. And accept them as the reality before which we must justify our existence. For this is the truth we must reach to live, that everything *is* and we just in it.

DAG HAMMARSKJÖLD, *Markings*

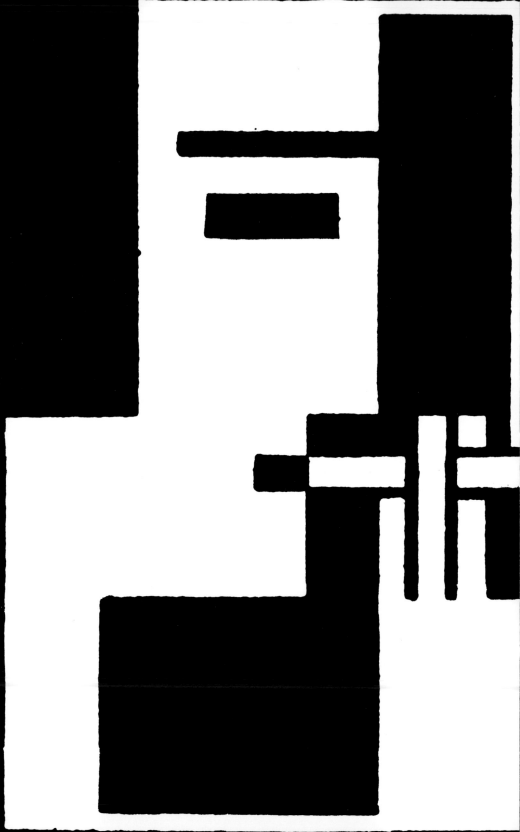

THE NO-DRAW RULE

Today a woman asked me if I could draw a mouse.

She spotted me in the window of the Blackbird Bakery, where I sat drinking tea in the middle of the afternoon with my friend the animal-rights activist. Kristin was just getting into my dog's anxiety issues when Meg blew in the door and asked me about the mouse.

Could I draw a Tasha Tudor sort of mouse? A mouse wearing a ruffled apron with lavender coming out of the pockets? Because her bed-and-breakfast, the Captain's *House*, needed a picture of its mascot, the Captain's *Mouse*, and looking through the bakery window, she had seen me and remembered that people said I was artistic and that maybe I could draw that mouse, you know, for money.

I nodded and smiled. Of course! I'd be glad to draw her a mouse. When should I get sketches to her? She told me and blew back out the door. I sat back, delighted, but slowly my moment of artistic exhilaration passed.

"How did this happen to me?" I asked myself in a hushed and somber tone. Only a few years ago I spent thousands of dollars to get an MFA in graphic design in order to fight my way bare-fisted down the concrete canyons of New York, hoping to make a bundle creating Citicorp logos while living in a Dan Friedman–like edgy apartment.

Yet here I am today, living in a cottage on an island in Puget Sound, talking about my dog's mental health in a café full of fleece-wearing baby boomers. How did I fall so completely off the design bandwagon? How did I get to the point of jumping at the chance to draw a mouse?

I felt bad. I felt wrong. I felt low. For you see, I am a graphic designer. And as a graphic designer, I am supposed to ride the crest of the technological wave while creating the information pathways of the future. I am supposed to provide workable solutions to communications challenges while educating the client about sustainability issues. I am supposed to lecture about the damning effects of the corporate control of the media to Seattle CEOs over Asian-fusion lunches at Wild Ginger.

But I don't do these things. True, every once in a while I get in a good jab about using less paper. And I can get riled and quote Voltaire at big meetings if I eat too many of those little cheese Danish from the coffee-service tray.[1] But mostly I just talk with designers and work with Web engineers, and go back and forth about copy with writers, and listen to the problems my clients are having with recurring lower-back pain or the new intranet. I spend much of my day hearing from accounts-payable people about where in the bill-paying cycle my invoice landed and why that will mean a two-week wait before a check can be cut. This is what it means to run a design business.

Sometimes I feel guilty for not riding the crests of those technological waves or paving those information pathways. Designers talk a lot about riding crests and paving pathways: they talk a lot at conferences

High Life

Sir Edwin Landseer, R.A.

Sir Edwin Landseer
High Life, ca. 1901–17

Taught by his father, Edwin Henry
Landseer first exhibited his paint-
ings at the Royal Academy in
London at the age of thirteen. He
specialized in portraying animals,
often dogs or deer, set in romantic
English landscapes. His pictures
became so fashionable that
Queen Victoria knighted him in
1850. After his death the mode
in painting changed, and critics
began to find his work shallow
and glorifying of violent sports.
Despite this criticism, Landseer
had a profound impact on later
British artists.

and in magazines about how important they are for doing so. But I've never seen a designer get up at an AIGA conference and give us the details of how she jumped at the chance to draw a small mouse in an apron and a little bonnet. Truth be told, I wouldn't want news of this mouse to get around. A mouse like this could topple my carefully constructed design persona, a persona of unflappable coolness and detachment. The grad students in the class I teach on "critical thinking for designers" expect me to stand at the podium, slightly bent with the responsibility of my large design concerns, looking vaguely exhausted as I check my Paul Smith watch to make sure I won't be tardy for my lunch date with Rem because of their long questions. They expect me to teach them about the values of the profession they are about to enter. Not just with my words but with my actions, with my attitudes. They take notes solemnly when I lecture about Barthes and Lacan, about C. S. Peirce and William James. They strive to understand my historical thinking, my critical stance, steeped as it is in modernism and postmodernism, in structuralism and post-structuralism. But what if they found out about the mouse—found out that *I* suggested the little bonnet?

Someone once asked an old Russian artist—a displaced person my father met after World War II—if he thought he could draw a dog, for money.

"They asked me if I thought I could draw a dog," he told my father, sullenly, and paused.

"So?" my father responded.

"Of course I can draw a dog!" the artist bellowed. "I was trained before the Revolution, at the Academy in Petersburg. I can draw *anything.*"

He could draw anything. Nothing was off-limits. Nothing was beneath him. But he was educated in a different time: a time before modernism.

Sometimes I think about that displaced old Russian, trained before the Constructivists, before the invention of graphic design. He was taught to draw birch trees and troikas and to live in a specific world, but—through war and destruction and upheaval—he found himself alone in a DP camp in Germany, family gone, house burned, friends scattered. Found himself still alive—still living—unvalued and bewildered, with no road home.

Perhaps all designers designing today are really displaced people. We live in the twenty-first century, but like that Russian artist, we were trained to live in another world. Our lost world is not one of birch trees and troikas but one invented a hundred years ago by people who dreamed utopian dreams. We live here, in our now. We design here, for our now, in a world that is as far from that utopia as *Bladerunner* is from *Pride and Prejudice*. We design for now, but we cling to the broken shards of other people's dreams for what the world could be.

Design education today is a modernist education. Now, when I went to grad school, I didn't know what modernism was. Oh, I knew that a sofa looked modern, or that a barrel chair was moderne. But I didn't know what the tenets of modernism were, I didn't know that it was a way of thinking, a way of responding to the world, in much the same way that Buddhism or Theosophy is a way of responding to the world. I didn't know that the modern way of thinking was a philosophy that hit Western society just before the turn of the last century,

Marcel Breuer
Wassily Chair, 1925
$1252

In spirit and stature, Marcel Breuer's Wassily Chair (1925) from Knoll has few equals. Believed to be the first bent tubular steel chair design, the Wassily Chair distills the traditional club chair to a series of strong, spare lines, executed with dynamic material counterpoint. The gleaming chrome-finished tubular steel frame inspired by the graceful, curving handlebars of the Adler bicycle is seamless in its assemblage. Thick cowhide leather slings create the design's seating surfaces, which maintain their crisp tautness for decades. Named for Wassily Kandinsky, the father of abstract painting and a colleague of Breuer's at the Bauhaus, the Wassily Chair is a symbol of the industrial heroism and engineering invention of the early twentieth century. Made in Italy.

—*Design Within Reach*

or that it hit not only in design but also in painting and literature and criticism and music. I didn't know that designers have no corner on modernism, even though we often think we invented it.

Objects hold ideas like amber traps insects. A sofa or a chair is an artifact of the time in which it was created, its lines and planes are what's left behind in the world when the storm of an ideology has passed by. But if we don't remember the ideas that led to the final form of the chair or the sofa, if we don't recognize the kind of insect trapped in the amber, the artifact loses all its meaning and becomes shape and line and form only. It becomes the narcissistic manipulation of outside things, becomes like a woman valued for her face who learns to ignore her heart.

The small Tibetan bell that someone gave me as a housewarming present is an artifact of a worldview. It's an artifact of a religion practiced high in mountains I will never travel, by monks I will never know. I like the bell's shape, and I keep it because I like the person who gave it to me, but its meaning is lost on me. Its cultural context is lost on me. My students could say the same thing about the Wassily chair.

The system of thinking that lies behind the design education of today is a hundred-year-old way of responding to the world. Sometimes it feels like its commandments were engraved on two big stone tablets, but those commandments were just the invention of a small bunch of men who created them in response to the times in which they were living. And though those tablets were thrown over a cliff in 1968, amid much talk about freeing design from modernism, no one in the next thirty years could find a really new way, a new system, for teaching someone to be a designer.

Oh, sure. Our students hear a little something about postmodernism, although we tell them that's all over with, so not to really

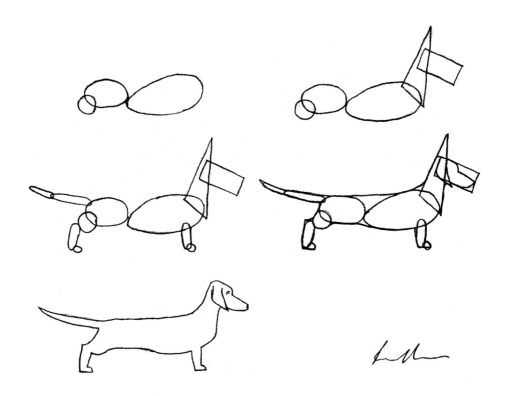

bother about it. And we have had a fine old time with structuralism and semiotics and poststructuralism and Marxism and a lot of other "isms" that, with a little tinkering, can be made to fit into design education. But the inculcated modernist commandments are still there underneath all we teach, holding up the design profession like schist holds up skyscrapers.

"What commandments?" you ask, annoyed. "I am my own person. I am free to do what I want. No one tells me what to design!"

And then you turn back to your computer and play around with altering an InDesign template for a while. And you pick type from the faces that Adobe bundled in when you bought your Mac and choose colors from the Pantone Matching System and feel insulted that I have questioned your independence.

Let's see. A commandment. How about this one: Graphic designers don't draw well.[2] That generality is a modernist convention, a modernist rule: the unspoken No-Draw Rule. Sure, we'll do a quick sketch here, a line drawing there. But we don't shade, we don't go in for realism, for perspective—for anything smudgy on gray charcoal paper. We never really *render*, as it were. Why is that?

No one ever actually said, "Don't bother learning to draw well." But most of your professors probably couldn't draw their way out of a paper bag. They can't do it: they look down on realistic drawing. And why is that? Because they themselves were silently discouraged from drawing well. The people who did not encourage your professors to draw were themselves not encouraged to draw by their professors, many of whom were refugees when the Nazis closed down the Bauhaus. Those expatriated Bauhaus designers didn't want their American students to confuse themselves with that lowly life-form, the *illustrator.* To a modernist designer, illustrators are people who just make things pretty on the outside. And those original modernist designers cared about what happened on the inside of a project, not just on the outside. Right? So why respect anyone who just tinkers with facade?

When those original professors of ours—those Bauhaus designers —came here, they brought their prejudices with them.[3] Their greatest prejudice was against middle-class living. They hated the "bourgeois," literally "the man of the provincial town," the comfortable middle-class burgher of 1900 who lived a life of Victorian restriction and sentimentality, who had a nice picture of a bathing nymph over the fireplace in his study, and who dwelled within the comfortable padded walls of the status quo.

The Bauhaus and the Werkbund and all those early modernist design groups did not want to be mentally linked to the illustrators who turned out nymphs. These designers liked to think of themselves as avant-garde, wanted to align themselves with the intelligentsia. They did not want to be in any way related to the fin de siècle, to the Academy, to the plaster cast, to the kind of person who copied reality instead of inventing a new one. Refusing to draw well was a way our design forebears could separate themselves from the bourgeoisie. Sort of like the female law students of the seventies who pretended they couldn't type so they wouldn't get stuck in front of a Selectric.

But today, we designers have forgotten the original reason that we don't draw well. We just somehow never get around to learning. We respond to an invisible prejudice embedded in our design culture, react to a stimulus we do not recognize, mold our lives with rules we do not see.

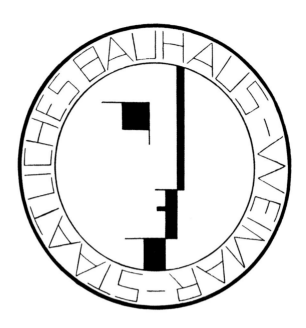

Oskar Schlemmer
Bauhaus seal, 1922

Vilmos Huszár
Advertisement for
Miss Blanche cigarettes, 1926

Very little drawn imagery
illustrates modern design, but
when it does, it is usually "constructed," rather than natural-
istic. In these two examples,
the human face is abstracted by
reducing it to rectangles, lines,
and planes.

So that's the No-Draw Rule. But there are so many more invisible rules—enough commandments to fill many stone tablets. Designers truly thought they were going to build a new world at the beginning of the last century. They were the ones who were going to make the rules for this new society. Even at the very beginning, there was ego in it. And here we are, one hundred years later. We've internalized modernist views without realizing it, and we respond to design problems with a very limited vocabulary from inside our invisible scaffold of rules. We may be in the "post-postmodern" era, but we are still just responding to modernism—not creating anything particularly new, just rearranging the deck chairs. Not creating a new language of design, just speaking the old language with a contemporary intonation.

I unwittingly followed the No-Draw Rule for years, casting an ironic eye on those who ignored it. I avoided every opportunity to play around with colored pencils, or to sketch an arabesque or a curling vine. I spent my time paring my work down to the essence, to the bones. I spent my time reducing everything to Frutiger and to line and vector and plane.

But you know what? After a couple of biopsies and a significant root canal, the realization that I will not live forever hit me at forty and with it the sudden knowledge that, by God, I *like* drawing little curlicuey things. I *like* soft colors and comfortable chairs. I enjoy the company of people who do not necessarily shop at Prada. I am just not interested in spending the rest of my life in the dogged pursuit of someone else's definition of perfection anymore. I am drawing that mouse, damn it, and no one is going to stand in my way.

This is not to say that I have lost my heart to sentimentalism. I do not mourn the unappreciated genius of Thomas Kinkade, Painter

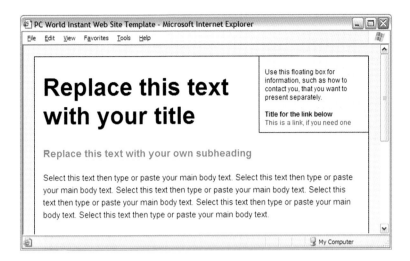

Tools like PC World's Instant Web Site Template—one of the plethora available online—give non-designers the ability to broadcast messages quickly and effectively. Although users can choose between one "style" and another, they cannot invent anything or change the rules of the system.

of Light™. Spiritual exhaustion and design burnout have not led my aesthetic sense astray. Rather, they have led me somewhere I had never traveled. I'm looking at things differently from the way I used to look at them. I can't help it—I'm looking under the rug. I want to see what modernism has hidden there.

This is not to say I am not an angry person. Funny people are angry people, and I am no exception. I'm sick of seeing regurgitated, tight little examples of seventies typography on design-department walls during grad crits and degree-project shows. I'm tired of the narrow language, the small sandbox, the limits of what we deem "good design." If I see another effort at ironic distance created with the tools of Swiss typography it will be one effort too many, and I'm going to wring that kid's neck. Or that of her professor.

Within my definition of modernism I include everything that springs from that movement—it and all its derivatives. Whether its precepts are taught wholeheartedly and earnestly or just as nostalgia and style doesn't really matter to me. The look is the same either way, the product is the same either way, the product's effect on us is the same either way, and I question its value to people.

I began this book because I had been thinking about my favorite subject—myself.[4] I had been wondering when it was that I first started to crave the dream of perfection that modernism offers us. I had been mulling over the fact that I spent most of my life trying to find that clean, pure, essential world; trying to get myself and my identity and my work under control. My rambling Anger at Self naturally gave way to rambling Anger at Context, and I began to think about how design, in which I have spent most of my life, supported my addiction to perfection so seamlessly.

How, I asked myself in this rambling anger festival, did I end up in New York for years, spending eighteen hours a day in a black-Formica-paneled design-office cubicle, breathing recirculated air, facing a glowing computer screen, which itself rested on a large expanse of black Formica that was to be "kept free of the clutter of personal para phernalia," according to the employee handbook?

How did design get me and every designer I knew to such an inhuman, soulless place? Why was breathing recirculated air and looking at life through sealed windows supposed to be ok for me?

above left:
Walter Gropius
Bauhaus Building, Dessau
1925–26

above right:
Conran Roche
Design Museum, London
1989

These two similar buildings with similar signage were designed and built more than sixty years apart. According to its Web site, the Design Museum in London is both the first museum "to be devoted exclusively to modern design" and "the U.K.'s largest provider of design education resources." The words "exposure to many points of view" do not spring to mind here.

Why did design's lack of support for me as a living, breathing person not matter? In what way, exactly, did working in a black Formica cubicle reinforce my value as an individual? Why was I required, should I want to be a designer, to spend my days—my life—in such a box, just because some downtown designer schooled in the modern thought all that black looked so damn beautiful?

The choices that designers and architects have made in the last hundred years silently mold us, silently direct us through the tunnels of Penn Station or up to the fifty-third floor of the Sears Tower. But they direct more than our movements. They direct us to notice one thing and not another, to value one thing over another, to identify with one thing rather than with another. As designers, we collude and unconsciously follow directions we don't even notice, created by the designers who went before us. Modernism—the guts of it, the strength of it, the egotistic beauty of it—carries with it effects we did not expect, and fosters attitudes about ourselves and others that may have been dandy in a utopia but do little good in our world.

How did design become the language and attitude and life that it is? When did we designers get the idea that reality should be arranged according to our views? Why have we not changed this idea, moved on with our thinking? For even after the disbanding of the Bauhaus, the disintegration of the International Style, the exhausting of postmodernism, we're all still chasing the perfect.

Gérard Bertrand
Franz Kafka chez Jacques Tati
2003
www.gerard-bertrand.net/pagetati.htm

With the creation of films like *Playtime* and *Mon Oncle*, Jacques Tati received accolades from the French intelligentsia for his bemused satires of the sterility and absurdity of the modern aesthetic. This image, once part of a Tati film, was digitally altered by artist Gérard Bertrand to include a repeated photograph of the author formerly known as a cockroach.

ch Ch

L

C

THE LOVE BUCKET

Graphic designers are born, not made. It's true, anyone can learn about design by rote, the way anyone can learn to dance by clunking his way through the *paso doble*, his nose in a handbook of steps. Books called *The Little Book of Logo Recipes* never go out of print for a reason: people need rules and systems—they need to know that they are doing things right, that their boss won't yell at them. But real dancing comes from deep inside the dancer, and real designing comes from deep inside the designer, and there's really just no recipe for that.

Designers are born with unusual sensitivities, and they design for one of two reasons. Those reasons often go hand in hand. And because I have so little time with you, I'm going to tell you simply that I believe people design from their deep love of the process of life or from their deep desire to keep that process at bay. Let us look at these two different types of designers.

Take the childhood behavior of a graphic designer and painter named Matt. When he was learning cursive script in grammar school, Matt had to be excused from writing the word "Egypt." The horrible look of that mixed bag of descenders was just too much for him to

bear. The word tortured him when he was trying to drop off to sleep at night, came back too vividly in the daytime. His mother finally had to write a note to his teacher.

After he had overcome the nightmare that was Egypt, Matt had a second problem. Making the flowing movement of cursive capital L's felt entirely beautiful to him, yet he had no L's in his name. Slowly it dawned on him that a girl in his class had not one but two capital L's in her name. He was torn up, jealous. He had no L's, and there she was with two. This time, no note could resolve the situation. Life, he realized, would be unfair.

As an adult, Matt went through a rusty-flattened-objects period a few years ago. There you'd be, minding your own business and trying to read the *Economist* or something, and suddenly he'd be standing in front of you holding up a tire-flattened beer can with such delight in his eyes that you would briefly consider mentioning the remarkable new advances in psychopharmaceuticals.

Then there's Tobias, a type designer. When Tobias was nine years old, he and his family flew to England to spend some time with his grandmother in Kent. In the morning, his mother came downstairs to find little Tobias sitting at the kitchen table, staring at a tin of biscuits. The rest of the children were outside yelling and climbing trees, and there sat Tobias, staring at a tin. After several moments of watching this, she woke him as from a trance. He told her that he didn't understand what made the tin feel so "British" to him, and that he was thinking it through.

Wisely, she faded into the background. And, after a while, he figured out that he only saw letters like these on things that his mother brought back from visits to his grandmother. It was the *letters* that made the tin feel "British." Gill Sans brought the *idea* of Britain into Tobias's ken, the notion of Britain being a separate entity, a separate consciousness from that of America. He sat at his grandmother's kitchen table for a long time, contemplating the wideness of the world.

When, as a child, you love the way writing capital L's over and over makes your hand feel, or you want to sit alone pondering a biscuit tin, chances are that you will be a graphic designer when you are old. You love the process, the texture, the feeling, the connotations of type and image. This sort of love is not unusual in those who go on to enjoy long, happy careers in design. This sort of thing never happened to me.

No. I was that other kind of designer. The one who wants to keep the process of life at bay. This is not to say that I did not fall in love with design when we first met. But "falling in love" is different from loving. Falling in love with someone means you spend much time using that person as a tall, narrow projection screen for all sorts of

National identity is often reflected
in the design of mundane objects.
In this example, even without Gill
Sans, there is no mistaking the
product's country of origin.

In 1931, Harry Beck, a junior drafts-man for the London Underground, created a plan for a new approach to mapping its railway. Using a simple diagrammatic method based on straight lines, he cleaned up and geometricized the mess that was London. The Manag-ing Director was not impressed. The plan was not implemented until—influenced by the recession of 1932 and wanting to increase ridership—the MD was persuaded to give it a try in 1933. The new map was immediately embraced by the public, and is still copied by transit systems throughout the world. The typeface, Johnston, was the immediate precursor to Gill Sans. Together these faces are ubiquitous in Britain, and comprise a de facto national typeface.

24

ideal images and wish fulfillments, while at the same time basking in images of yourself as expressed by said Other. Having spent so many years in various degrees of this psychotic state, I do not deny its deep appeal. Mania just feels so darn toasty. But loving is different, and involves helping people throw up, or being proud of them when they do kind and invisible things, or putting up with the way they use "hopefully" incorrectly because they put up with the disgusting way you spit out the toothpaste after brushing your teeth. It is a different state entirely from falling in love and should be described with another word, but here the English language comes up short.

I remember the moment I fell in love with design for the first time. My love object was a book. "New" textbooks at Wilston Elementary usually saw quite a tour of duty before they got to Mrs. Dye's third-grade class. But this book really was new and a bit oversize and slim, and I remember cracking it open slowly for the first time and smelling fresh ink. It had a laminated cover the color of ripe apricots, and the inside pages were bright white—smooth, filled, and uncoated. How soft that paper felt when passed along a nine-year-old cheek.

Yes, that book about the world of tomorrow comes back to me again in all its freshness: Proust's madeleine has nothing on rotogravure. A social-studies text about our wonderful future, that book erased catastrophe from the list of cultural options. Its sixties-modern architect's renderings of schools and airports and parks all floated in pages of pristine white space. I wanted the world it represented: I wanted to walk into that world. The little puffs of trees all the same. The little men and women gathered in ones and twos in plazas and on sidewalks. The fountains, frozen in midspout. That world of tomorrow was a vision of the future that stopped time, that explained life and cleansed it. Such a vision was very calming to a kid who often crouched under her desk in the suburbs of Washington, DC, palms sweating, while the air-raid siren wailed a drill.

Love and fear. Freud said they are the two calls to action. Because of my basic dislike for the man who made sexuality a synonym for illness, I don't spend a lot of time quoting Freud. But I like that particular idea. People who grow solidly into their place in the world design to express their astonishment at its beauty, their comfort in their natural sense of that place, their love of that place. People who do not feel that they belong in the world as they find it design to create the world as they know it could be. They want to create a space for themselves in that ideal world. They want to create a foundation for themselves, the launching pad they should have had.

I'm thinking of Tom, an architect. In the woods behind his family's suburban house on Long Island, there was Tom, at ten, building forts. You couldn't get him inside in the summer. He built forts connected by trenches—entire trench networks connecting entire lines of defense. Now he designs big houses. Now he has people working for him and a big, clean office and good clients. Now he advises people to cover their exterior walls in shingle siding to keep the Nantucket winds from buffeting their thirty-thousand-square-foot vacation cottages. But if you ask him about happiness, he will tell you about lying on his stomach in a dugout fort in the woods in summer, his clothes smelling of fresh earth and grass, his small self unseen, gone to ground, safe in its network of trenches.

One designer celebrates life, the other searches for safety from it. Some people delight in a flattened beer can's improbable flatness, others understand the beer can's perspective: can imagine the snow tire above them and the hard road below and, in short, have been afraid. That kind of designer is an anxiety-fighter and takes delight in complexes of structure that will make things work better, make a safer or more cohesive world. That designer responds not to the world's beauty but to its chaos.

Now, think for a moment, and you will recall that people who try to control things are fearful people. We who try to run the world are just trying to make sure that nothing bad happens. We aren't sure that we can take what life dishes out. So we do our best to make sure that life doesn't come up on us unexpectedly. We like to get a clear view of what's coming down the highway ahead of us, and one of the best ways to do that is to design the highway.

Looking back at design history, we can put each designer we come across into one of two buckets, the love bucket or the fear bucket. I'm not going to do that now, though it would be wise for you to carry those buckets with you to the next lecture you attend on design history. Personally, I think the love bucket is the bucket to be in, if you can possibly arrange it. But it takes a wise and strong designer to pull herself out of the fear bucket (strength not unlike that of life coming out of the sea). It takes a wise and strong designer to elbow his way rapidly over the dust and flop into the love bucket. Not many of us are that wise or that strong. But back to design history.

BROWSING THE TOME

Today, when I was waiting for the tea water to boil, I found myself at the living-room bookcase, paging through those big picture books that designers love to publish about each other. After looking at the Tibor Kalman book again and the Alexey Brodovitch book, and after thinking that I should call Sears and ask them if my propane stove should really take this long to boil a damn teapot, I came upon my well-worn copy of the Tome of Famous Graphic Designers, one of the big books that tells students in design-history classes about who went before us and about who, therefore, we are.

I found myself stuck on the pages that chronicle the work of Walter Gropius, one of the very first modernists, and that led to my rummaging around for the Tome of Famous Architects, so that I could look at who architects say he was, and meanwhile the tea water boiled, and I absentmindedly turned off the burner. I began to think about Gropius not as the icon we all studied but about who he actually was before he became an icon. I began to wonder what urged him to design, what drove him to make things. I found myself thinking that since he was in on the beginning of things, since he is such a lauded designer, and since he exerted such an influence on design in its infancy, what urged him to design might well tell us something important about how we design, and how we came to believe what our role should be as designers. If I could figure out the way he looked at the world, I might find a good place to jump into my search for the origins of our design perfectionism. By then, the tea water was stone cold. I had to start all over again, this time holding a tea bag in my teeth so as not to forget my main mission.

Here are three important things about Gropius's early life. First, he was Peter Behrens's assistant and shared studio space in that office with Adolf Meyer, Mies van der Rohe, and Le Corbusier. Second, he served with distinction as a German cavalry officer during World War I. And third, he founded the Bauhaus, a radical reorganization of the Weimar School of Arts and Crafts, right after the war.

When you read those three facts, you may have skimmed over the second one because it seems to have so little to do with design. But go back: it is the most important fact of the three. The first fact is preamble; the last is response; but the middle one contains Freud's call to action, the designer's call to action, the change that insured Gropius's everlasting place in the Tome. If ever there were an experience that could change a nice, self-satisfied, middle-of-the-road Socialist designer into an evangelical utopian idealist, serving at the front in World War I would be that experience.[5]

Some people don't know much about World War I. It seems so long ago, and yet it's not. My grandfather, the same man who sat and listened to me conjugate Russian verbs when I was thirteen, fought in World War I. But when I look at my students, I know that that war is as far away to them as the Crimean War is to me. It's history: they recognize the name, it's dusty and vaguely familiar, but it's not related to life as we live it now. Yet for designers, that war is very important. It destroyed so much that it created the opening for a basic change in the way life would be lived in the West from then on.

Here's a quick summation: Ten million soldiers died and twenty million were wounded in the four years of "the war to end all wars," which was declared in 1914. Those numbers don't include the civilians who died, the children caught in cross fires. At the Battle of Verdun alone, a "battle" that went on for six months, 350,000 Frenchmen and 330,000 Germans died: 680,000 people. That's about 3,778 people killed a day—that's one World Trade Center a day, for six months, in one battle. Verdun—one battle in a long war—killed the equivalent of every single person in Manhattan.

Imagine coming back to your nice Victorian home after that. Imagine having just lived through four years of watching your friends die hanging in the tangled barbed wire of no-man's-land. Imagine yourself, hunkered down in your trench, listening to them scream all night until the screaming stopped. Imagine coming back home after that, putting on a dinner jacket for Mama's evening musicale, and listening to a matronly soprano singing "The Last Rose of Summer." How were you supposed to sit on your little gold ballroom chair, wearing your dinner jacket and sipping your *digestif*, after what you had been through, pretending nothing had changed?

The rift between Victorian culture and the realities of the war was just too big. That war made Gropius a reforming zealot. It made his friends reforming zealots. They would do anything not to go through that blood and chaos and futile misery again. And they blamed the Victorians for a lot of what they saw wrong in the world. They hated Victorian sentimentality. They hated the stuffiness and facade of bourgeois society. They hated the falsity of society as they knew it, and they wanted a radical change in the way society worked. They wanted to clear off the table with the sweep of an arm. "Start from zero," as Gropius used to say, erase the slate, begin again. Nikolaus Pevsner, a historian of art and architecture, says,

> It is the creative energy of this world in which we live and work and which we want to master, a world of science and technology, of speed and danger, of hard struggles and no personal security, that is glorified in Gropius's architecture.[6]

Gropius wanted to master the chaos of the world, master the danger and the strife that are part every human life. Pevsner just loved the moderns. Look at that quote: He's loving the idea of mastery over science and technology, speed and danger, hard struggles and the base camp blown apart just when you're up climbing the mountain peak. Pevsner's Gropius is a James Bond who climbs the glass curtain wall, meeting danger head on. Pevsner sees him not as a person but as an action hero—an action hero who set out to build the world again, according to his own lights. We see him that way, too. We designers love a hero.

When I was a kid, my family recited poems after dinner. Not that I grew up in *The Cherry Orchard* or anything—it was the late sixties, and we lived in Virginia at the time—but we didn't have a TV for quite a while, and we had to do something with the relatives, who were quite the mixed bag. The Russians on my father's side liked poems, as did the Southerners on my mother's side, and in my family, if you didn't have a few poems under your belt by the time you were nine,

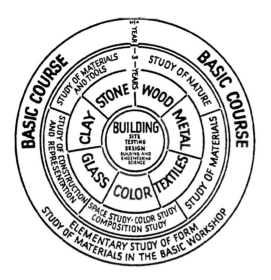

Diagram of the Bauhaus curriculum, 1923

Using the notion of "building at the core," the Bauhaus compartmentalized and charted creativity in order to "master" the human design response.

well, eyebrows went up. If the evening were the right kind of evening, warm on the screened porch, we'd sit around and quote poems back and forth, over the candles, and lean back and look at the stars, and the young cousins would practice falling in love with each other, while the older Russians would think privately how fine it was to be alive and warm and not sitting on a train frozen to its tracks in Siberia, and the older Southerners were thanking their lucky stars that the Depression was over and they weren't eating sweet potatoes for breakfast, lunch, and dinner.

They always started off with a few Pushkin poems, and then one by Tyutchev or Baratynski, and then all the non-Russian speakers would rebel and someone would quote *The Canterbury Tales* or read something by Archibald Rutledge. But after Chaucer and a child's getting through "When, in Disgrace with Fortune and Men's Eyes," a general murmur would go around, and someone would urge my father to recite Matthew Arnold's "Dover Beach." He recited it the way Russians of his era recite poems—not ponderously, in the stentorian tones of an actor, like so many Americans do. He recited it with a quiet, throwaway air, as if the scraps of the words came to him from nowhere—as if he were just thinking them up right then, a man speaking his own truth.

Now, if you have pretensions toward intellectual subtlety, particularly if you, say, got your creative-writing degree at Columbia twenty years ago, you will have inherited a pseudointellectual sneer toward "Dover Beach." You will consider it too-oft quoted, and you will tell me that you are far more interested in the minor poets of the time. This, my dear, is your problem. If you get "Dover Beach" out and read the whole thing, you'll find in it the basic philosophical problem of the modern era. You'll find in it the fear that "design" was created to solve. If you are a designer, in this poem you will find the major problem of your working life. Parse "Pictor Ignotus" all you want: you won't find your major life problem there.

Something in the timbre of Pevsner's writing about Gropius reminds me so much of the end of "Dover Beach" that I must quote the final stanza of the poem for you:

Ah, love, let us be true
To one another! For the world, which seems
To lie before us like a land of dreams,
So various, so beautiful, so new,
Hath really neither joy, nor love, nor light,
Nor certitude, nor peace, nor help for pain;
And we are here as on a darkling plain
Swept with confused alarms of struggle and flight,
Where ignorant armies clash by night.[7]

34

Arnold wrote this poem in 1867, almost fifty years before World War I. But that sense of having been abandoned by a patriarchal God, the creepy feeling that life might be essentially meaningless, was already floating in the air forty years before the Bauhaus.[8] Modernism had been burbling along in the thinking of the intelligentsia for some time. But after World War I, shocked by the war, many people felt the world changing under their feet, and the change scared them. The rise of science and the decline of religion had left a big gap where psychic comfort once had been.

Some people ignored that gap and tried to go back to the way life had been before the war—the way some people would probably try to go back to American life if Manhattan suddenly blew up. Other people tried to fill that gap, that shell-blasted crater where the comforts of religion and Victorian sensibilities had once stood, by creating new structures in which to believe. And all of this happened not so long ago. Not long ago at all. My father was born in the middle of it, my aunts in the early part of it, my grandmother before it. And I'm not that damn old.

Gropius and his friends fought against anxiety and meaninglessness, fought against the dull, futile ignorance they had seen all around them at the front. They felt the futility that Arnold felt. But instead of turning to human connection, to love, as a path out of the darkness, the way Arnold did, they chose to build a new world out of the mud, to build a utopia that did not admit death and disease and rain and trenches and blood, did not admit the primal, brutal, unkempt side of people. They just pretended it wasn't there.

Modernism in design wasn't inevitable. We were not destined by some larger force to design the way we do. Our design language

Both of these typographic configurations were created at the Bauhaus, but one of them looks "more Bauhaus" to us than the other. The top example, created by Lyonel Feininger in 1921, reflects a different design philosophy than the lower example, designed by Joost Schmidt in 1929.

Gropius and his like-minded colleagues won the political battle that raged between expressionists and modernists at the school's inception. History is written by the winners of conflicts, so we know the Bauhaus for its rigid geometry, standardized forms, and machine aesthetic, not for its expressive energy.

wasn't the only choice on the table at the beginning of the last century. It is easy to forget that when the Bauhaus was forming, a fight broke out between the Expressionists and the moderns, and—after a great deal of political maneuvering on Gropius's part—the moderns won. You don't hear so much about the Bauhaus Expressionists or the illustrators who put up such a fight against Gropius's views. Like the Gnostic faction of Christian believers, they were hounded into oblivion by the orthodox faction for not believing the "correct" thing. And our history was written by the orthodox.

In the first Bauhaus manifesto, Gropius says:

> Together, let us desire, conceive, and create the new structure of the future, which will embrace architecture and sculpture and painting in one unity and which will one day rise toward heaven from the hands of a million workers like the crystal symbol of a new faith.

Let's remove chance from the equation; let's create a unified future that will not admit error. Let's organize every controllable facet of life so we will not have to face the meaninglessness that we feel in the dead air all around us. Let's create the future before it takes us down.

Now, I ask you. This man who started the Bauhaus, this great patriarch, one of the greatest influences on design in our time, did he design from love or from fear?

And if he designed from fear, and if your professors' professors learned from him, in which bucket are you swimming?

HOME, PERFECT HOME

A few months after I moved to the island where I now live, I got a call from a woman, a project manager at a huge software company, who had heard me speak at a conference. She was sharp as a razor and funny and honest and had liked my speech, all of which I found very appealing. Her design team created and maintained the company's Home of the Future installation. Her engineers thrived on hearing new points of view. Would I do a workshop about what the word "home" means?

Now, trust me. There aren't too many purely semiotic gigs out there, and I love a project that doesn't end with me actually having to make something. So I said I would be glad to do a workshop, and she was happy, and I immediately started thinking about what a "home" really is and reading Witold Rybczynski and looking things up in the dictionary.

Because of a completely different situation, I was also in the middle of reading Ernest Becker's *Birth and Death of Meaning*, a tour de force of interdisciplinary synthesis. It is the kind of book that colors all your thinking when you are reading it, and I do not advise reading

it if you cannot afford to have your thoughts dipped in a dye bath of someone else's brilliance for a time. However, I did not know this before the Home gig.

So there I was, reading about when bathrooms got incorporated into the house and wondering what the full quote actually was for Le Corbusier's "a house is a machine for living" chestnut and generally going along on that tack. I was thinking I'd breeze through this workshop, leave the team members with a few PowerPoint bulleted items about a house being "something that serves as an abode" and a home being "the physical structure or portion thereof within which one lives, as a house or apartment." And then I'd go downtown to Nordstrom's, take a nice, long look at the shoes, have chicken farfalle in the café, and get a large check a few weeks later.

But I hadn't counted on the insidious nature of Becker. And I hadn't counted on this woman's giving me a detailed tour of the Home of the Future installation a few days before I was to run the workshop.

To get to Seattle from my island you have to take a ferry. I have a large spaniel with long fluffy ears. And I maintain a large garden. For these reasons, my '89 Aerostar is not always, shall we say, detailed. In fact, the driver's seat got ripped by an edger, the back seats are encrusted with spilled liquid fertilizer, and at least one rake and three boxes of soil amendments are jammed between the front seats.

On the day of the tour, which was to spur my mind on with ideas for the workshop, I did not think about the condition of my van as I drove off the ferry and toward Redmond. Nor did I give a thought to my dog's being in the back seat. I was thinking about traffic and about what I would see at the installation. I was thinking about what the Home of the Future would be. Because of a low tide the ferry docked late, and I had to floor the van to get to the appointment on time. Flooring the Aerostar gets it up to almost forty-five miles an hour. As the time got later, I began to get nervous. Now, when I get nervous, my dog gets nervous. In order to help me drive, she jumped up to the passenger seat, peered nearsightedly through the windshield, licked her dry lips, looked at me worriedly, and urged me along with moans. I would have played soothing music at this point, but the radio has not worked since 1990.

I took the off-ramp, made the turn at an alarming forty-three miles an hour—all turns are alarming in a wheeled refrigerator—and careened into the software giant's big circular drive. Suddenly, the Aerostar, the dog, and I were in a completely different world, a city-state of huge, new, numbered buildings. Every car parked along the new drive was a new car, every sidewalk a new sidewalk, every lawn a new lawn. The young engineers playing touch football on one of those lawns wore brightly colored fleece jackets and new chinos.

I missed the building. I couldn't read all those little numbers so fast, and as we went around the circle drive again, my dog and I looked anxiously at each other and then peered out of the windshield again, simultaneously. Finally we got into the right parking garage. Getting out of the van, I brushed the dog hair off my minimalist zip-front pant-suit, rearranged my underwear slightly, applied some lipstick using the side mirror (making that owl-like expression women make when they are checking their eye makeup), and hurried out.

When I entered the visitors' building—an entire separate structure in which this company corrals "off-campus" visitors—the woman I was supposed to meet stood on the other side of the security barrier.

"How did you know I was here?" I asked.

"We've been watching you since you entered the drive!" she said, and busted up laughing.

So that's what those signs in the garage had meant about video surveillance.

Anyway, I took the tour. The Home has a front door, just like a real house. Since the front-door handle is intelligent, it unlocks at the touch of a familiar hand. However, my hand was not familiar. There's a little thing in the front door that reads your retina and opens the door if your retina has been scanned. But my retina had not been scanned, and the little thing wasn't working that day anyway, so we just went in. When we entered the foyer, all the shades in the house started to go up, the lights went on, and soothing music began to play. All well and good. I have seen retina scanners and automatic shades before, having lived in a hotel for some time, so I was OK so far.

Well, it's been a couple of years now, and I can't remember all the things that acted automatically to welcome us in. But I do remember my

CHANNEL1

CHANNEL2

CHANNEL3

CHANNEL4

AUTO

2005/08/02 23:0

Wisecomm

Matti Suuronen

Futuro House, 1968

guide's saying that her engineers designed around the daily require-
ments of an invented Home Family. And I recall her going over to
the kitchen counter's computer screen to monitor how the traffic was
doing on the Renton S curves and to program the timing for the Family's automatically defrosted and microwaved dinner. The appliances
and entertainment systems all stored and retrieved information on
the Home's Web site, and I remember her showing me where the
Home's Children were at that moment, according to the GPS matrix
on the screen.

The tour went on. First, the living room, with its cineplex-size
projection screen, its entertainment options all stored on the Web site,
its deep, screen-facing tuxedo sofas covered in expensive, honey-toned
fabrics. In that living room, a person could see or store or re-store or
find any movie ever played on any cable channel—could play or save
or list on the screen any song ever recorded or sent over the airwaves.
Then I saw the dining room, with its soft, neutral beiges and padded
dining chairs, with its sideboard that supported a full range of communication devices and its upholstered walls, on which hung electronic art that changed with the press of a button. After that, I viewed
the festively colored children's room, which featured complete computer suites and parental video surveillance. All in all it was the perfect
Home. Except, come to think of it, there wasn't a bathroom.

Driving back to the ferry in the van with my dog, I felt sad. I felt
sad, and I felt lonely, and I knew that if ever I were forced to live in
that wired-up gizmo of a place, I would surely go mad. For a home is
not a habitat.

I drove to the ferry terminal and parked, and my dog and I took
a walk around the periphery of the lot and stood together waiting for

the ferry to come in, and it got blustery and dark, and that's when I started to think about Ernest Becker. In his book, the book I had been reading, Becker doesn't mention design or houses or anything. But he does think for a long time about what it takes to be an individual, to be a fully realized human being. This is what he says:

> The great tragedy of our lives is that the major question of our existence is never put by us—it is put by personal and social impulsions for us. Especially is this true in today's materialist, objectifying, authoritarian society, which couldn't care less about a person answering for himself the main question of his life: "What is my unique gift, my authentic talent?" As the great Carlyle saw, this is the main problem of a life, the only genuine problem, the one that should bother and preoccupy us all through the early years of our struggle for identity; all through the years when we are tempted to solve the problem of our identity by taking the expedient that our parents, the corporation, the nation offer us; and it is the one that does bother many of us in our middle and later years when we pass everything in review to see if we really had discovered it when we thought we did. Very few of us find our authentic talent—usually it is found for us, as we stumble into a way of life that society rewards us for.[9]

My dog and I got back in the car, and I ran the heater, and I thought about what Becker said and about the four levels of power and meaning that he thought a person could choose to live by. First, he thought the basic level was the personal—the person you talk to

The AIBO® Entertainment Robot understands and responds to more than one hundred words and phrases, which are taught by the owner as the robot is "raised" from puppy to adult. At the initial release of AIBO® in Japan in June 1999, all of the three thousand units sold out within twenty minutes. More than one hundred fifty thousand units are currently on the market worldwide.

when you are alone, the secret hero of your hidden life. The second level is the social, your intimate circle: spouse, close friends, family, dog. The third level he calls the secular; it is your allegiance to a larger social group, a nation or a party or a corporation, your devotion to science or art. And the fourth, the one he considers the highest level of power and meaning in a person's life, he calls the sacred: a person's connection with "an invisible and unknown power, the insides of Nature, the source of Creation, or God."[10]

Sitting in the van with the windows rolled partway down to reduce the carbon monoxide buildup, it hit me that a real home—not an electronic showplace but a home—is a place where Becker's four levels find physical support. In a real home there's a place for talking to yourself alone. There's a place for your visiting friend and for her children who climb all over your sofa while eating pudding. There's a place for stuffing envelopes for the campaign or settling in and reading Gibbon from first volume to last. There's a place to sit and look at a tree or a leaf and to think uninterrupted thoughts about that tree or that leaf. In short, a real home supports a person's individual power and meaning. And the Home that I had just looked at supported neither of these things. The Home I had just seen supported ongoing, inevitable entertainment, continual communication, constant surveillance. Where was the room for the silence you must not be able to flee, the silence you must endure and survive if you are going to wrestle any idea to the ground? The silence you need if you are going to have your own ideas?

Waiting for the ferry to come in, I thought about how designing the way we do has affected the ways that people lead their lives today. And I wondered how growing up in the Home of the Future would affect the ways our children visualize themselves, their future, their potential. That Home asked them to learn in very specific ways, but are those technological skills going to help them develop as individuals? Or is the real design to keep the Family watching, responding to stimuli and entertained, so that it learns only what it needs to keep the juggernaut of a technological, consuming society moving along?

Most of my working life I assumed that designers were designing to create a place where a person could stretch as far as possible and become truly individual. But I believe now that design is actually a field in which the welfare of humankind, the alleviation of human suffering, the betterment of individual lives, and the support of individual identity are rarely considered. Modern design never set out to support the individual. It set out to support anonymity and universality, to clean out those nasty slums and put up some nice projects instead. It set out to get inappropriate people out of the street and appropriate people high off the ground. Sure, there was always an architect or two who wanted to do something surprising or fantastic, but that person was always eventually criticized for not heeding the demands of "reality." The cold, hard, clean demands of reality: A reality of surveillance and security barriers and separate buildings for strangers. A reality built on fear.

I drove onto the ferry and parked the van, turned off the engine, and looked out at the black water and the lights of the harbor, waiting for the boat to push off from its moorings. I thought again about the idealism of those early designers. They believed that the order they were imposing was the right thing for mankind. They believed that order outfoxed chaos, that they could bend industry to right practice, to good use. But was the Home of the Future what they had in mind?

This poster, featuring a manicured poodle cleverly inserted into an archival photograph of Mies van der Rohe's iconic Farnsworth House, was designed by prominent New York design studio Bureau to announce a Parsons School of Design symposium on the professional enmity between architects and interior designers.

Members of Parsons's interior design department objected furiously to the poster, claiming that using a poodle to represent interior design once again reinforced an antiquated stereotype—that designing interiors is the joy of the frou-frou poofter, whereas designing architecture is the sacred duty of godly men in ties.

This strange collusion between idealism and industry? Surely the engineers who design the Home are idealists. They are bright and full of energy and believe that what they are doing is lots of fun, and valuable, too. After all, who *wouldn't* want to know what her children are doing upstairs in their rooms? Why not just flick a switch and find out?

Together these engineers and designers "desire, conceive, and create the new structure of the future," just like Gropius would have wanted. They "embrace architecture and sculpture and painting in one unity," just as he had hoped. But this unity rises toward heaven only as far as a satellite hookup, and it rises not from the hands of a million workers but from the hands of a very small number of very intelligent, very highly paid, new-car-driving engineers dressed in fleece and chinos.

This technology that early designers believed would save us from chaos and blood, this universality that designers have supported and made attractive to consumers since the beginnings of design: What is the price we have paid for it? Yes, everything is crisp and clean and efficient and fast. But crisp and clean at what cost to independence, to individuality, to self, to spirit? Sometimes designers have used industry as a way to make their ideas real in the world. But sometimes—more times, it seems to me—industry has used designers to make its purposes look ideal.

Perhaps you want to live in a world in which, because of media-instilled fear or your own compulsivity, you can look at a live image of what is going on at your front door in Tulsa when you are standing on a street in Tokyo. Perhaps, because you have not been taught to think broadly, or you are afraid to think broadly or to be alone, you believe you *want* to spend your life being entertained, receiving messages, responding with your wallet, monitoring your kids, checking your messages from the dining-room console. Maybe you are thinking to yourself, "She obviously doesn't understand the thrill of being an early adopter." Please. Turn off your cell phone, turn off your laptop, turn off the TV and the music system for a moment, and let me tell you a little story.

In New York I went out for a year with a guy who turned out to be a psycho, but for most of the time this was not obvious to me. In the evening he'd call me and ask me to come down and see him. I'd get up, put on a coat, walk down to his apartment, and go up in the elevator; after a ring of the bell, he'd unlock the door without a word and be back on his sofa, propped up with pillows, before I could get inside. This always felt warm and welcoming.

He'd sit there till late at night, every night, changing channels on two huge TVs, keeping track of other shows with TiVo and one-touch dialing people on the phone just to find out what they were watching. The more anxious he felt, the faster the remotes clicked. You can imagine the delicious sense of inclusion this behavior instilled in me, the live visitor. As he clicked and whirred, I did the dishes in the sink or read a magazine or two or watched the TV's blurred reflections—the blues and whites and magentas—dance in the huge black windows of his studio.

He could have been an attractive man. And, truth to be told, when he was not clicking and dialing he could pull off a creditable imitation of being a person. But when he was sitting on that sofa, changing channels compulsively, his face slack, you got a full dose of his true character. And that character was empty and isolated and terrified.

Since designers are bound up with industry, we never consider what people really need to be whole people or what the collusion of design and industry has offered them instead. We create devices that distract people from thinking, from working through the fear that accompanies real thinking, from coming out the other side. We help to make people believe they can't live without movement, communication, distraction. We teach them the exact opposite of the truth.

Wondering about all this took me far out of the Aerostar. I came back to reality as the ferry pushed forward, and I sat for a long time, feeling it gain speed heavily, watching it throw its white bow-wave high in the black water. Partway across the sound we began the long starboard arc that would bring us to the island. Feeling the turn, my dog lay down in the back seat. She put her nose on her paws and sighed, knowing we were going home.

DOING PENANCE

I did a very dumb thing recently, but I blame it on the design decisions of others and refuse to accept personal responsibility for the huge mess into which I got and into which I dragged innocent bystanders. I never meant to upset anyone. But I did, I did—and now I have paid the price.

When you run design workshops at a lot of different schools the way I do, you discover early on that one way to get absolutely nothing done and to be blocked at every turn is to blow in from nowhere—a stranger with attitude—and be prissy and demanding to the Graphic Design Department Secretary. For this reason, when making hotel and travel arrangements, when trying to get paid or be reimbursed, I have always adopted a kindly, congenial air that I believed convinced said staff member of my affable nature. This facade is a micron-thin varnish applied to my true anxiety-ridden personality, but it generally gets the job done. Department Secretaries don't go looking for trouble. But when trouble comes to them, they are prepared.

I was scheduled, as I have been regularly for a few years now, to give a lecture and run a workshop at a prestigious design school in the autumn. I love doing the workshop, I love the students, I love seeing the faculty, and I generally consider the trip one of the high points of my year. I get to see the fall colors and so on and reacquaint myself with area restaurants and go for at least one walk to admire the cobblestone streets and Federalist buildings near the school.

I am a woman of habit. Every year I stay at the same place, a nice old cell block of faculty housing made just for visiting people like me. The halls are bathed in fluorescent light; cobalt blue commercial-grade carpet covers the floor; and the bathroom and the kitchenette have an industrial feeling conveyed by wall-mounted towel dispensers and blue linoleum squares buffed to a high shine. The rooms are private as a tomb, clean as a laboratory, and the thud of the doors and the click of thick deadbolts give me a secure feeling in a town known for its petty crime.

This year, I came straight up from two weeks in New York on a late train after a day with a key client that could only be considered hair-raising. "Oh, by the way," the client said, "I'm leaving, my assistant is leaving, and I know we are your only contacts here, but don't worry, I'm sure that after the reorganization of the marketing department, you'll be at the top of the consultants list." This sort of aside can give a person with a mortgage a sudden numbness on the left side of her body. But I made the train, and stowed my computer, my large bag of books and papers, my purse, and my rolling suitcase—a suitcase suitable for airports, not cobblestone streets—above my seat. The trip was fine, though I stared at the red plush of the seat in front of me the whole way, wondering if anyone I knew would want a used dog when the bank foreclosed. It was 11:00 PM by the time I arrived.

After a short cab ride from the station to the campus police to pick up my key, I trudged down the steep hill to the visiting-faculty-housing cell block, various bags draped over my shoulders, pulling the bouncing carry-on over the stones. I got up the stairs to the door and tried to put the key in the lock. No go. I tried again. Nothing. After a bit of rummaging and fumbling, I found my reading glasses and in the light of the street lamp realized that the key was not for my good old familiar quarters but for a place called Richard House, which was on a street I thought I might have just rumbled past.

I'll spare you the bitter details, but after a good half hour of rumbling uphill on wrong streets and asking very young students about directions on a remarkably nippy night for September, I found Richard House. Clearly, someone had just bequeathed it to the school. It looked so recently bequeathed, in fact, that I wondered if they had removed the body yet. It was a nice old house from the outside, all sorts of Victorian gingerbread and peeling white paint. The porch seemed solid enough, though the front door was rickety. Its lock had the equivalent of a trick knee, and it took my key a few times round before I could push myself, loaded like a camel, into the foyer.

I looked around. Straight ahead, a child's bureau, covered in stickers, sported one of those Mediterranean-style lamps found solely in motels. To the right, a powder room with mixed fixtures featured metallic silver and light blue flocked wallpaper. An industrial TV and two dorm-style cobalt and walnut-veneer chairs stood in the center of what had been the dining room, lit by a bare bulb above. Homey. I slowly got up the stairs, various bags hitting the old railing softly but strongly enough, I thought, taking a look at the missing spindles, to bring the whole thing down in a heap of splintered wood and dust.

My room was marked clearly with one of those gold, stick-on numerals, and I entered it to find one of the most unappealing and dismal places ever seen by a tired, roving faculty visitor with worries about Chapter 11. Two children's bunk beds, unbunked, stood stripped of sheets on opposite corners of what must have once been a lovely nursery. Two dressers, one white French Provincial from Sears circa 1969, the other industrial-strength beech Formica, stood together in unresolved duality on one side of the room. Thoughtfully, someone had put an industrial beige metal locking cabinet containing three thin wire hangers on another wall, in lieu of a closet. And then, of course, there was the obligatory nonworking candlestick lamp with ballerina-tutu shade standing on a wooden biology-lab table. The room was bathed in the light of a single, overhead, fluorescent fixture the size and shape of a giant glowing breast. No phone. No TV. No heat. No radio. No alarm clock. As I describe it, it seems to have a certain monkish charm. But trust me: it didn't.

I am a tall woman. I haven't slept in a regular twin bed since 1977. And the prospect of sleeping on a kid's bunk the night before a large presentation filled me with such self-loathing and homesickness that I sank down onto the unmade mattress, buried my head in my hands, and cried about how I could have had a real career and some company to pay my health insurance but no, I had to be a design critic and look where it had gotten me. And I worked myself into such a rage of tears and snivel that I lost what was left of my head and made the mistake for which I have now paid penance and for which I am truly sorry and promise never to do again.

It was midnight. But because of someone's brilliant design decision to create and market the cell phone, particularly the cell phone in which one can store numbers that are then available at the touch of a button, I found myself dialing the office of the Graphic Design Department Secretary. As I say, it was not my fault. Had the cell phone not been invented, I would not have had one and would not have had the opportunity to make such a rash move. Luckily, she was not in at midnight. All I remember is hearing a beep and then letting loose a stream of epithets that could have made the proverbial sailor blush, if not given him a permanent case of rosacea. Gone was my veneer of camaraderie. Gone was my people-person affability. I remember barking something about having seen crack houses more welcoming than this, that I was afraid to be alone in this creaking old firetrap dump of a building, and to get me out of here pronto. Then, calmed by my letting loose this load of abuse on the head of a person I did not know, I fell asleep in my clothes, curled like an infant on the bunk bed, under the bluish glow of the giant breast.

The next day, I woke up after a lot of sleep and things didn't seem so bad. Birds chirping, sun streaming in, that sort of thing. I figured out that I could drape myself over the two bunk beds if I aligned them vertically. And I called the Department Secretary to say not to worry about changing where I was staying because I could make it work. Her voice, a bit on the clipped side, said that they had already made other arrangements and to bring my things to the office. Something in her tone chilled me. Loaded with bags, I bumped slowly down the hill, dreading the worst.

"We've been unable to find you a motel room," she said coolly. "But the Department Head has offered to put you up for the rest of your time here. She and her husband live a half hour away by train. There are three or four trains a day. I'm sure you'll be very comfortable."

She smiled. I smiled. She turned back to her computer screen. I briefly considered impaling myself on her letter opener.

It is important for you to know that the Department Head, a quiet, charming, and brilliant woman whom I barely know but actually like, is married to a Famous Photographer whom I also barely know but actually like. The idea of staying with people I barely knew yet liked was appalling to me, because it meant I had to be nice to them and be a good guest, rather than just spend my off hours swanning around half dressed watching junk TV and ordering chicken Ceasars from room service in some moderately priced hotel, as had been my plan.

And it wasn't as though they were thrilled with the prospect, either. The Famous Photographer coming down, as he was, with flu-like symptoms, and the Department Head having to go to some posh Friday-night thing in New York. But they, ever elegant, bore up. And I smiled and smiled and took a faculty friend up on his offer to give me a ride there my first night.

Dusk was falling and a soft rain drifted in and out as we drove the half an hour to the Head's house. We talked about design and about the vicissitudes of business, and it didn't seem long before we turned into a wooded residential area and rounded a bend to come upon the most beautiful contemporary structure I have ever seen. In the cold and rain, the building's translucent outside walls glowed from the lights on inside; the whole house looked like a lantern set down on a wooded bank. My friend dropped me off and drove away. I bumped my bag to the door, feeling distinctly down-at-heel and ill-suited to be staying in such a perfectly beautiful place with such perfectly success-ful people.

"We should go out to dinner," the Photographer had said on the phone before we came up, "because we really don't keep food in our kitchen."

I assured him that I had eaten, and he seemed relieved. And when he opened the door, and I got my first look at the blazingly polished cherry floors and took off my shoes and padded along behind him in my socks as he gave me a tour of the design studio and the photo studio and the wing with the bedrooms and guest quarters; when he told me that he had powder-enameled two of the inside walls to match his beech trees' fall foliage; when he explained the air-recirculation system and warned me not to try to open the window because the windows didn't open; when I saw the inside of the Sub-Zero and beheld one Brita pitcher and a six-pack of Coke and nothing else at all; when I focused on the various modernist chairs set in minimalist groupings, I knew that the Secretary of the Graphic Design Department was not only angry at me but that, in fact, she wanted me dead.

She wanted me to die in a dust-free environment with a security system and a charming host, far away from anything that smacked of reality, far from anything that could give me a sense of my own identity, of the worth of that identity. I didn't like the falling down Victoriana of Richard House? I didn't like a little imperfection, a little edgy, nervous-making real life? Well, then. How about staying in a germ-proof lantern with no fresh air for a few days? Huh? How about camping out in a place that is so clean, so beautiful, so thought out, so complete, so filled with impossibly valuable simple objects that you will lie in the guest bed and feel the weight of all that design pulling you down like the stones Virginia Woolf put in her pockets as she waded into the river. That'll teach you to dial my number on your speed-dial at midnight, you visiting-faculty ingrate.

62

But as I say, I have learned my lesson. It won't happen again. Never have I been so happy as on late the second night, as the Department Head and I waited for the train to go home to the Lantern, when the Amtrak announcer suddenly came on the loudspeaker and reported that someone had jumped in front of the train a few stations down the line, thus suspending service for a few hours. Never have I been so filled with joy as when the Department Head turned to me and said, "Perhaps we should put you in the Marriott tonight."

Do not call me hard-hearted when I say that person did not jump in front of that train in vain. I kissed my way down the hill to the Marriott. I taught well the next day because of that person. And because of that final jump, the Department Head rejoined her husband, who drove down and picked her up, handing me my bags, by then almost comatose with the flu and charming as ever. They

went home together, and I believe they had at least a few hours alone before their next guest arrived, during which, perhaps, they drained the Brita carafe with real relish, toasting the modern aesthetic.

I mention all this because most of the next morning I sat in that Marriott and pondered the Lantern and the designer's urge toward abstraction. I wondered, What makes us crave simplification, makes us want to get something down to its elemental structure? What makes us want a Parsons table rather than a Louis xv bombé chest? What is it about how we expect to live and what we expect to value that guides us in these decisions? And that's when I remembered that little book by Wilhelm Worringer.

The completion of most Ph.D. dissertations doesn't usually cause much of a stir. After the flurry of printing the book, one copy goes to the school's library, another to the department, and a third stays on the top shelf of the writer's bookcase in an expensive archival box. Every few years the dust is blown off the box, the box is opened, and the writer marvels at how long the thing is and wonders why he can't remember writing any of it. This, however, was not the case with Worringer, who completed his dissertation in 1906 at the ripe age of twenty-five, saw it published as a book in 1908, and spent the rest of his life writing prefaces to new editions.

You haven't heard of him, or of his book, *Abstraction and Empathy*, because he is not talked about in design circles, though what he had to say caused a great deal of commotion in the painting and literary worlds of his time, and he has been quoted and thought about ever after in these fields. When I found him, I thought it odd that no one in design had ever suggested I read him. But as I began to think about his major thesis, I realized that there might be a good reason why he is not much talked about in design. His book is not about the clearly defined ideology we call "modernism," because in 1906 there was no such thing. Worringer finished his dissertation a year before Picasso painted *Les Desmoiselles d'Avignon*, and he didn't mention the avant-garde in his discussion of Western and primitive art. But his stance was modern, he saw art in a different way from the critics who had gone before him, and he said two things that concern us as designers.

First, he said that representational art—a picture of a hillside with a cow standing on it, for instance—gets its power from "an objectified delight in the Self." Seeing it, we are able to identify with the cow or the field. We are able to say, "That cow is a lot like my cow. That field is a lot like my field." And we feel confident in the world as it is, we feel surrounded by known cows and fields, and we feel safe. And because we feel safe, we find the picture beautiful. Worringer also said that the urge toward abstraction is the opposite of this "delight in the Self." He believed that, in historical periods of uncertainty, people want to abstract objects from their context—want to wrest them from life's unpredictability. In anxious times, people want to transform what they behold in the natural world into absolute, transcendental forms. So, one pole of art-making is the urge toward empathy, the other pole is the urge toward abstraction. Worringer saw all of Western art as slung between these two poles.

You and I, as designers, can take Worringer into our history and see that the search for essence, which is the quintessential modern design agenda, is a direct response to the anxiety and unpredictability of the time in which modernist design was created. We designers hug the pole of abstraction in the high wind of reality. And perhaps this is why Worringer is not much quoted by designers. What designer

1896   1984   1988

The Prudential logo has gone from realism to modernism and back in the last 110 years. Its original logo, from 1896, featured a realistic drawing of the Rock of Gibraltar, denoting strength, solidity, and imperviousness to change. The logo remained largely unchanged for the next ninety years.

In 1984, it was "modernized" and made so abstract that many clients did not know what it symbolized. A sinking building? Flooded factory smokestacks? To many it looked like an iceberg. (Design note: Using a huge piece of ice that floats around unmoored, hides most of its bulk below the waterline, and sinks large ships may not be the best way to define a company.)

In 1988, Prudential took a step back, moving away from high abstraction and to a recognizable image of Gibraltar that could inspire an empathetic response in its clients once again.

wants to admit to responding to the anxiety caused by life's unpredictability by seeking immutable forms? What designer wants to admit that by making clean, elegant designs for brochures and Web sites and buildings and facades he is only covering up what Worringer calls his "immense spiritual dread of space?" Oh yes. Being expert at covering up spiritual dread is going to look great in the old company brochure. Let's put that up there high on the résumé.

If we agree with Worringer's thesis of the two poles of artistic creation, we can see that modernism was not just "a search for new forms" the way we were taught in design history. It was not just "a pushing away of the Victorian matriarch," as some historians see it. It was:

> ...an urge to seek deliverance from the fortuitousness of humanity as a whole, from the seeming arbitrariness of organic existence in general, in the contemplation of something necessary and irrefragable. Life as such is felt to be a disturbance of aesthetic enjoyment.[11]

For people who want their straight lines to be straight, life itself is the problem. The modern urge is the urge to get away from organic existence in general. It's a negation of life. It's a fear of life. Perhaps, without knowing it, without thinking about it, that's why some people choose to live in beautiful lanterns, to breathe recirculated air.

GOODBYE TO SADNESS

I went up to Providence to get my master's degree in graphic design in the early nineties. I figured that moving from New York to Rhode Island would be the way to break up with my boyfriend without his noticing. This did not turn out to be the case, and he called my bluff by driving up one weekend and breaking up with me, with a certain hatchetlike directness, in a McDonald's parking lot.

So there I was in Providence, a grad student in my thirties. I moved into a small apartment in a house that had been built in 1792. It had wide-plank floors, a hearth in the kitchen and another in the living room, and my two neighbors were friendly. Downstairs, directly below me, lived a lithe young woman whose cat often got out, prompting her to go about the building whispering "Kitaj, Kitaj," which I thought very urbane. And on my floor, across the center hall, lived a trim, elegant man in his forties who seemed terribly mature to me, worked some sort of quiet nine-to-five job, and often played a sedate flute after he returned from work. I enjoyed this new living situation enormously after having battled cockroaches, crack-addicted neighbors, slumlords, and other vermin in New York for so long. My Providence landlord was mild mannered and thoughtful, Transit

Street was peaceful, Kirk's flute twittered like a sleepy bird in the evenings, and the summer before grad school came softly to an end.

I looked forward to slipping comfortably back into the academic world after so many years in New York, and invested in a pair of trim jeans and some snug T-shirts that I thought made me look, if not young, at least active. My plan was to keep my best clients going on the weekends, to get back in shape by working out for hours each day, to take long walks in the autumnal Rhode Island woods, to read Proust, buy lovely old Windsor chairs, and enjoy a respite from the real world of bills and bus exhaust. But things did not go exactly as I had planned.

As it turned out, grad school was hard. I had not expected this. No coasting, no vacationing, no sleep. True, I had been running my own design firm, but I had no education in graphic design, knew nothing about it at all except what would sell, and had to get in four years of formal training during the same two years in which we grad students were trying to piece together a skeleton from the random bones of cultural criticism being thrown at us by various professors. So much for keeping the clients; so much for the luxurious workouts. In my two years in Providence I never took one walk in an autumnal wood. I bought no Windsor chairs and read no Proust.

Grad school was nothing like the mental spa I had imagined. I was terrified most of the time. Terrified that I wouldn't get it right, wouldn't be good enough, that I might break a rule—break one of those rules that was not supposed to be broken, rather than one of those rules that was supposed to be. I couldn't tell the damn difference, though everyone else could. They all blithely ran around doing clever ironic subverting things while I trudged through the dust of mediocrity in thick-soled shoes.

I was wise to be fearful, because I was in way over my head. The design language these people spoke was a foreign language to me, a language of exclusion, and I wandered about in a strange land, blocked and dumb as a post. Providence was nothing like the sedate Federalist town I had thought it was. (A dicey-looking man cornered me in my doorway one dark night and offered me his blackjack, just in case I should ever need it when walking home. I briefly considered using it on him.) And perhaps strangest of all, my neighbor—the quiet man, the flutist, the nine-to-fiver—turned out to be a speechwriter by day but an abandoned and decidedly libertine jazz saxophonist by night. I found this out abruptly very early one Sunday morning, during my second REM cycle, and lay there in my bed, astounded, listening to jazz pour out of his saxophone like crude oil from a gushing well.

After a brief interlude of adaptation, it turned out that I liked music. I liked it better than I liked design. I liked to be around the people who played it better than I liked to be around most design-ers. Musicians weren't interested in what you looked like on the out-side. They wanted to know what you could do when you picked up an instrument. I liked the way musicians treated each other better than the way designers treated each other. I was too old to be a groupie and too poor to be a patron, but I loved to hear these people play music and spent a lot of time in Kirk's wicker chair listening, when I was supposed to be in front of a computer tweaking type.

Kirk's friends knew that they had long ago ceased to be inter-esting to record companies and that anything resembling a career was not open to anyone who played jazz. They were not interested in going over to Fusion, they were not interested in light jazz. They played standards and listened to Shostakovich, and they liked blues and Beethoven and sat around listening to Rachmaninoff's third con-

HUB CAP/FREDDIE HU

ulian priester/jimmy heath/cedar walton/larry

certo, shaking their heads. Sometimes very young musicians would drop by to hear them when they played and sit on the floor, silent, as if witnessing history.

I thought a lot about music when I was living in Providence. And I wondered why I was so much more comfortable with musicians than with designers. Like design, jazz was a hundred years old by the time I found it. And like design, it came of age in the twenties, the heyday of the American moderns. But unlike design, it bubbled up from the country's unconscious. It was not sanctioned by an industrial society looking for a new facade in the way design was sanctioned. Jazz did not claim to be building utopia, it didn't look like it was doing much good for anybody, and it didn't seem to care. Jazz was an affront to the established order, and people were afraid of it.

Black people played it; young white people went to hear it. This was bad. White people started to play it. This was worse. The music was a mixed-up pile of allusions and feelings, like the country was then, full of quotes and riffs, and it gave voice to the confused time in which it was created. It gave voice to the uncontrolled side of America, to the side that Mother didn't want to see. The people who played it bathed in joy and hardship and pain and alcohol, and they still do. European designers, who were busy making rules about what the new reality should be, unconsciously tried to control the deep sadness and anxiety their countries felt after the war. But American jazz musicians played id to that ego, made music from memory and instinctive impulse; they improvised immediate relief and satisfaction.

There's an old story about Zoot Sims playing in Denmark. A waitress comes up to him and says, "Mr. Sims, would you like to try our Danish beer? It is called Elephant beer."

And he says, "No, baby, I drink to forget."

They drank to forget, and they played to forget, just like those German World War I veterans designed to forget. These musicians I knew in Providence had different things to forget, but they played to forget them, too.

Late at night, after they'd finished their gigs at various restaurants, they'd come over to Kirk's and sit around in his living room and play music. Gray Sargent would be there, quoting on his guitar; and Jack Menna would bring over his charcoal grill and his drums and work back and forth on both instruments. I'd come over, too—sleep was pretty much moot at that point—and eat and listen. When they played, they sat in a circle and watched each other, listened to each other and played a solo or melted back into the background, supporting someone else. They'd step in and step out of a tune, sure as girls playing double jump rope. And at the end of a song they did the oddest thing: they laughed. They didn't laugh because something was funny—it was as involuntary as a breath. That laugh was an appreciation of all that had just happened, right then, there in Kirk's living room, in the middle of the night. I have never heard a laugh like that go round a room of designers.

Unlike design projects, which are still generally created in a strictly hierarchical way,[12] music is a language of inclusion: it can't exist without cooperation. Everyone has to play by the same rules and keep the same time, but, aside from the bandleader, everyone is pretty much equal. Unlike music, design does not happen in time but out of it. Design does not exist in the moment—it yearns toward the future, always. The lag between our dream of the future and the future itself guarantees that we will be unsuccessful. By the time a building is built, the reality it was constructed to respond to has changed. By the time a Web site is up, parts of it are obsolete, and 1.2 is on the rails.

INDESTRUCTIBLE

dar Walton / Reginald Workman **ART BLAKEY**
& the
Jazz
Messengers

By the time the catalogue is printed, the light blue sweater is sold out. Design hides from the present by planning the future, but the future doesn't always cooperate. Music makes use of the present—it fills the present, leaving no room to think about past or future.

At first jazz was the music of New Orleans and funerals and Carnival. During Prohibition, it became the companion of organized crime and speakeasies and alcohol, cocaine, and heroin. But after World War I—there's that war again—it had the same run of good years that modernist design had. You can chart them on the same graph, jazz and design. Starting with their beginnings at the turn of the century, then a first heyday in the twenties, then one in the thirties and one in the forties, and then a brilliant finale in the sixties, followed by a dismal seventies and watered-down eighties. You can chart them on the same graph because they are related: both are antidotes to a sensitive mind's encounter with the brutish, meaningless parts of life. Perhaps they are produced from the opposite sides of the brain, or from ego and id, or from Jungian "masculine" and "feminine." But both design and music are *responses*; they're like the secretions that oysters make to keep a grain of sand from bothering them—secretions that we value, and call pearls.

Unlike design, which gave its founders large medals and many luncheons, jazz saw many of its brightest stars die of kidney failure, of overdoses, in car crashes. Though, now that I think of it, Brodovitch died alone and alcoholic in his brother's guest bedroom in France. But then, he was a Russian.

In Providence, in the daytime, I read my Philip Meggs and went to design-history lectures and sat in six-hour crits and learned how to make design and, perhaps more important, learned to criticize it. But at night I learned the history of jazz music and blues long before there

THE RUMPROLLER
LEE MORGAN

WITH JOE HENDERSON   RONNIE MATHEWS   VICTOR SPROLES
AND BILLY HIGGINS

STEREO
THE FINEST IN JAZZ SINCE 1939
84199 BLUE NOTE

were PBS shows to codify that history. I heard stories from people who had played with Artie Shaw; I heard about how Benny Goodman played his last sessions with a whiskey bottle balanced on the music stand, about how Art Pelosi backed into a swimming pool once while playing at the Dutch Inn in Galilee, Rhode Island (proving that not all saxophonists walk on water). I heard a young saxophonist describe his violent attack of nausea at the prospect of playing for Dexter Gordon. I learned about time and about ears—"good ears" and "no ear"—and that music is as much about listening as about playing. And I began to wonder why designers are not taught as much about seeing as about making. Perhaps we don't want to see too much.

The musicians I met in Providence had very few things. Their life was lived on the inside, not the outside. They dressed in whatever was on sale at the thrift store, and they didn't pick things for their retro look. None of them drove a car that had been manufactured in that decade. Many of them were on the road to full-blown alcoholism, because most of life was spent waiting to play, spent in psychic attitudes of relative pain, in the hair shirt of reality, and alcohol or painkillers seemed the next best thing to playing music. It was not a pose: they had no money. Among them, it was not unusual to see a perfectly beautiful woman missing one of her back teeth or a man who had walked from his house in North Providence because he didn't have bus fare. Once Kirk invited everyone back to his apartment after a show only to realize, as people trouped in, that the only things in his refrigerator were two eggs and half an onion.

In my other life, the life of the design studios, the people I knew wore clothes from Banana Republic or Prada, with the occasional vintage piece thrown in for effect. (Vintage clothing is expensive, and not particularly related to thrift.) If they drove cars, they drove Passats and Volvos bought during their former lives as art directors. None of them needed dental work. All had figured out how to pay for the education that they knew would put them on the map of their chosen profession. The lonelier I felt surrounded by designers, the better I felt surrounded by musicians. Music was the antidote to my modernist education. It was my escape and my forgetting.

Toby and I often stayed late in the design studios at the school on weeknights. He liked the night; it kept people from bothering him, and he worked best in silent hours. I felt too dumb to make anything in front of anyone, so I liked to be in the studio late, when other people wouldn't be looking over my shoulder. This made us companions, he on one floor and I on another, and usually he was the only other person in the building. By the time we quit and I dropped him off at his apartment, the sky had lightened to a dull grey.

Once, after a late June night in the studio, I drove home down Benefit Street as the sun rose over the river. Yawning, I made the left onto Transit Street and turned into my driveway. It was still so early that no city noises greeted me when the engine stopped—no hum of traffic or clatter of garbage men; no cars starting up or tread of feet on the sidewalk. The old houses stood, shouldering together, wrapped in their night silence. The dew lay thick on the grass, and the lemon balm I'd planted near the driveway stood motionless, winking in the sun like a semaphore.

I got out of the car stiffly, thinking of breakfast and bed. Slamming the car door I heard something, and looking up, I felt notes from a quiet guitar drifting down on me, like petals from a burst rose. Someone was still playing music, upstairs in Kirk's apartment. Someone had played all night and was still playing. And I knew who that someone was. What were the words to that tune? I could hear the singer in my mind, telling about her heart's deep sadness, telling sadness to leave her forever, urging her heart to sing again.

I walked up the stairs and looked into the open door of Kirk's apartment. Jack, the drummer, eyes shut, sat upright, breathing rhythmically in an easy chair. A horn player lay on the sofa, head thrown back, his instrument still held firmly in one hand. I couldn't see Kirk, though I heard a familiar snoring through the open bedroom door. Gray sat there alone playing his quiet guitar, the only one awake in the sleeping house.

Framed in that soft light, that light of new leaves, Gray made his slow way through "Tristeza." He didn't hurry. He didn't lag. Perhaps he played for the sleeping musicians, knowing they heard his music in their dreaming; perhaps he played for himself, or for no one, or had forgotten that he was playing. Listening to him as I leaned against the doorway, tired from the night, I forgot about fear and worry. I forgot about designing, about controlling everything. I forgot to fear the future. I stood happy in the present when Gray played his guitar.

GONE WITH THE WIND™

NO SOFAS

A few years ago, before I left New York, I was so broke from writing a book and not doing business that my friend Tom, the architect, took it upon himself to help me get some corporate writing work. After a couple of brief phone calls, he clicked his cell phone closed and told me to go over and see a cutting-edge designer acquaintance of his who was running a furniture company. This guy, he assured me, was the *dernier cri* in furniture design, was starting to get recognized in the design press, and would surely have a need for a little high-priced PR. I put on my sensible separates and went over.

At that time, the meatpacking district in New York was just being discovered. Big, relatively cheap spaces could be had there, and during that strange couple of years it was not unusual to see a few sides of beef hanging in front of some new photography gallery, while a trash can on the corner burned brightly. I got out of the taxi on a pretty rough block, some sort of furtive deal going down on the corner, and I was glad, again, for being so darn tall and not an easy mark. I found the building and buzzed to be let inside. The lobby had been gutted, but quite a bit of meat still hung somewhere in the place, because it had that cold-blood smell of walk-in freezers. But when I asked, the security guy in the foyer told me that, indeed, there was a furniture company on the seventeenth floor and to go on up. I picked my way around the stripped I-beams and found the elevator. It was a dark, iron elevator, a big suspended box with gates, suitable for holding racks of swinging carcasses, and I stood in the middle of it as I ascended, not wanting to touch anything.

When I got out on seventeen and came around a corner, I found myself in the brilliant light of a huge floor-through loft. The entire place looked as if it had just been scrubbed down. Not a speck of dust. The huge windows sparkled, the scoured cement floor, unrefinished, provided a perfect "imperfect" contrast to the white-painted brick walls. It felt like a birdcage suspended high over the city, with the Hudson River shining below the western windows, and the buildings of downtown crowding the southern exposure. And yet, after my eyes adjusted to the light, I noticed that for a furniture company the loft held a distinct lack of furniture. As a matter of fact, there was absolutely nothing in the white expanse except—and I had to squint across the loft to see it—one aluminum Parsons table. And behind the table, in an aluminum chair, sat a man. I decided, from that great distance, that it was a man because he stood up when I entered. Thank heavens for contextual social cues.

I lumbered for what seemed a long time over the concrete floor toward the Parsons table, loaded down as I was with overcoat and outsize carryall. And when I finally drew up in front of it, breathing heavily, the man kindly offered me his chair, because there was no other chair in the loft. As I sat down, feeling suddenly loud and slightly too warm in my gray flannel, the man asked me polite ques-

84

tions about whether I'd had a hard time finding the building and if it was still cold outside. After waiting a decent period for me to stop trying to get comfortable in the aluminum chair, he leaned back on the aluminum table, his full black-leather trousers creaking softly, and introduced himself. He was, in fact, the president and CEO of the furniture company.

I had pretty much figured this out, since there was no one else in the loft, but he seemed to think it important that I not confuse him with a receptionist, so I feigned surprise and enthusiasm over finding out his true role. He started talking about why he had started the company and about a $10,000 black-walnut side table he was just producing and about what he thought design was and this sort of thing, and he really was a very charming guy, and at some point we went to the all-white laminated kitchen tucked around a corner and he made me a nice Illy espresso. I was just standing there, mentally calculating the price of his trousers and of his black cashmere mock-turtle and adding it to what his cost per foot must have been, including escalations, when he suddenly said, "I had a customer come to me the other day and ask me to design a sofa."

"Oh?" I said.

"Well, you know. I just laughed. Just laughed!"

Here he chuckled in a dry sort of way, so I chuckled dryly, too, having no idea what was so damn funny about designing a sofa.

"So you don't design sofas?" I asked, in a leading sort of way.

The designer looked at me and let out a low moan. He leaned heavily against the wall near the espresso machine. His trousers creaked mournfully.

"People sit on sofas," he said.

"People sit on sofas," he said again, "so I don't make them."

"I see," I said. But I didn't see. It was a while till I saw, and Tom never did understand why I never did any writing for that furniture company.

It would be fine to base design on a great quest for perfection if Web design and sofas and buildings were bounded by a large chain-link fence that divided designed objects from people. But in our world, people and objects are all jumbled up together. People, ugly and fat and appalling as they can be, are going to sit on the sofa you make. They are a necessary component of the design process, and the design that ignores them and their real lives is not design but fetishism.

As designers, we have been taught to love the object, love the completeness of the finished masterpiece. But because we have paid so much attention to the outsides of things, we have forgotten the insides. This is pretty ironic, considering that the early modern-ists were so very interested in the outer form expressing the inner essence. We have learned to treat ourselves as designed objects and to get frustrated with ourselves because we are never complete, never whole, never finished. Increasingly, because of our training, we treat other people as designed objects, too. The consumer society in which we live is doing its best to foment that frustration; it reminds us con-stantly of our incompleteness, our unphotogenic imperfection, and our consequent valuelessness.

We flip through magazines and try to look like what we find there—but most of us can't ever be the beautiful twelve-year-old so valued by the sellers of products. We cruise Match.com and know that if this guy doesn't work out we can toss him because there's bound to be a better-designed person out there, one who has all the qualities

we have written on our list of desired attributes. In searching for the perfect mate, we go through more and more people in shorter and shorter periods of time and treat them more and more like objects and less and less like individuals. We look for the perfect one, and the perfect one never comes. And why are we doing this? Why are we doing this when our parents never did this and our grandparents never did this? Because we have been taught to expect perfection, to desire only the perfect, and to discard anything that does not measure up. We have learned to turn our backs on people and things that do not achieve our impossible standards for beauty, for value, for worth. Never confuse modernism with humanitarianism.

You know, when a person has the habit of treating people as objects to be used for his own fulfillment, to be used up and digested and excreted, we call that person a narcissist. That's the real psychological definition of narcissism. It's not just selfishness; it's when a person believes that his body is the boundary of the universe, and

Theo van Doesburg
Counter-Composition XIII
1925–26

At a glance, van Doesburg's painting seems the ultimate expression of an art based on geometric perfection. But if we look closer, the artist's hand is evident in the brushwork, and the painting's age revealed in its cracks and chipping paint.

that all other bodies or minds or objects exist to satisfy his needs. And what does our current modern pose reflect, if not that? Even our efforts at embracing imperfection include rules. We embrace the beautiful imperfect, but not the kind of imperfect that wants to move in with us and throw his socks all over our tufted wool carpeting. But what have we got, in the last analysis, if we have only perfection? When something is perfect, when something is perfected, it is finished. It is complete. It is dead to change, to the world, to life. What are we so afraid of that we are constantly trying to put the brakes on life, on change, on difference?

Designers have always been choosers rather than creators. Traditionally, we put things together—type and image, brick and steel. We don't fire the brick or extrude the steel. We don't take the picture or design the type. And it strikes me now that, in our wake, our whole society is fast becoming a society of choosers. Creation, for the average below left:

Gerrit Thomas Rietveld

Zig-Zag Chair, 1934

executed 1941

below right:

Maarten Baas

"Where There's Smoke"

Zig-Zag Chair (Rietveld), 2000

Though modernists hate to admit it, designed objects have always been commodities. Rietveld's iconic Zig-Zag chair is available today in many forms at many price points. Original versions have sold for over $40,000. Can't afford an original? Buy a contemporary copy for about $500. Still too pricey?

Buy a mini version, about 3 inches tall, for $114. Feeling wealthy and iconoclastic? Buy Maarten Baas's toasted and epoxied version, one of an edition of twenty-five, at Moss for $3,900.

 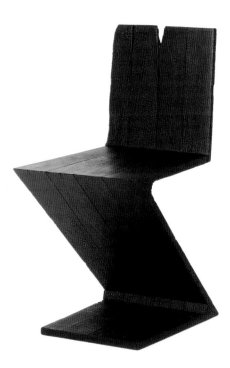

Andy Warhol
Before and After No. 3, 1961

American pop artists often appropriated imagery from contemporary culture to comment on society. In this piece, Warhol used a found drawing promoting the benefits of bodily perfection through plastic surgery.

person, is a lot less necessary and a lot less attractive than it used to be. We don't carve an old stick on the back porch. If we want a stick that looks like we carved it on the back porch, we buy one at Cost Plus for nothing; we pick from the three sticks they offer. We don't make a dress out of old curtains à la Scarlett O'Hara, we buy a cheap one at Target. We choose the red one or the green one.

We've been choosing more and more and creating less and less for some time now, but I am just catching on that in becoming a society of choosers rather than of creators, we are becoming a society of people who take the passive role: the traditionally female role. Increasingly, we're leaving the driving to others. We are leaving the fine, feathered display, the "choose me to be your mate" role, the traditionally male role, to the corporations that purvey products. It's like the old sex dance of penguins or of cockatoos, and we are the quiet one, the silent one, the female one, and the producer is the showy one, the one who offers, the male one. What will happen as we—both men and women—shift from expressing ourselves individually by making things into expressing ourselves only by choosing? What will happen to us as a culture when we have been completely conditioned only to choose between options, rather than to come up with solutions?

And if we are about choosing and not about creating, and if the palette of responses continues to narrow as consumers vote with their cash for whitened smiles and cinnamon breath, and as other, less-successful choices are dropped from the purveyor's roster of available options, at what point are we still actually choosing? At what point are we just jostling along like a cow down a slaughterhouse chute?

DODOS IN FLEECELAND

I lived in Manhattan for sixteen years, but two years before the World Trade Center bombing, I left New York for good. I didn't plan to leave. I intended to continue living my designer life—nice clients, nice shoes, nice restaurants. But because of an unfortunate misunderstanding, in the resolution of which it became apparent that I was not actually the holder of the lease for the apartment in which I had been living all those years, I suddenly got evicted from my one-bedroom-living-room-and-kitchen-with-separate-dining-room apartment on West Seventy-ninth between Columbus and Amsterdam and found myself living month-to-month in a nine-by-sixteen-foot studio on West 103rd high over the Hudson River.

I have been thrown out of college, left by boyfriends, and fired from jobs. None of these is a nice experience, but being evicted was worse than all the rest. I was suddenly without my center, my known haunts. I did not know my neighbors; I did not know the checkers at the grocery store. In New York, being evicted is like being shunned, in the way that old religious sects used to shun people. Suddenly all backs turn against you. In a big city, that shunning is not personal, and that somehow makes it worse.

However, I was handling it. I had my faux fireplace. I had my Regency mirror over the faux fireplace. I had large vanilla candles in front of the Regency mirror. And that was about all that I had. If I had had a TV, perhaps none of this would ever have happened. TV keeps the walls away from us. But my TV was in storage.

One evening an old friend called up and said he thought I should come down to his place for a while. I was annoyed that he called me. I was in the middle of my evening routine: watching the blue twilight haze come off the river. It was the hour that the French call *l'heure bleue*, the time of night in early spring when the whole world is suffused by blue—the sky and the water, the fog off the river, the tugboats and barges, the trees of Riverside Park, the people walking home from work, all blue. I find blue very soothing. So I said graciously that I was doing fine and not to bug me. He said he would order in that fake sesame chicken that I liked from Empire Szechuan. He mentioned how much I loved sitting out on his terrace and looking at Central Park in the morning. The whole thing did start to sound a bit like a vacation, so after much cajoling, I said I would come down.

He was on to me, but I didn't know it. I had been managing very well with my new technique of keeping fear at bay by not going outside. It wasn't that I was afraid of being outside. It was that I was afraid that that weird thing would happen again in some unfamiliar place.

Perhaps this has happened to you. Maybe you were once minding your own business, standing in a bank line at the corner of Forty-second and Sixth, thinking of the usual money worries and client worries. And perhaps suddenly, gathering height from nowhere, a wave of fear rose in front of you—a huge wave of fear, a tidal wave—and it came across the lobby at you with such force that you knew you were going to be swept backward and smashed into the side of the manager's cubicle. You wanted to run, but you didn't know where to run. You couldn't remember your name or what you were doing in a bank or what a bank was for. Perhaps this has not happened to you. Oh, that's right—it happened to me.

The fear of that panic happening again kept me inside the little room at West 103rd and the river, had me ordering in lunch and dinner, had me watching the blue of the evening, every evening. You'd be amazed how New York made this possible. What with delivery by grocers, dry cleaners, and all kinds of restaurants, the phone, computer banking, e-mail, fax, FedEx, and kava-kava tea, I was keeping the consulting business running and the book progressing without ever going out.

Nobody noticed for months. My boyfriend at the time, the mediated psycho, sensed trouble brewing and took a powder a few days after the bank incident. My mother had just died, so she wasn't checking up on me. Friends called, but I just rescheduled dinners over and over, and since I do that a lot anyway, it didn't seem that odd to them. I never thought about the fact that I never went outside. I just never went outside.

But Burt wanted me to come down to his place and was insistent about it, so I set my mug of kava-kava down on the counter and put on some sunglasses, even though it was evening, because sunglasses made me feel safe. I looked like a drug dealer with Texas hair. Dressing wasn't a problem because I was already dressed. I had been dressed for some time—three or four days, at least. After the bank incident, I had decided that it probably wasn't in my best interest to sleep and had given away my bed. I spent my nights fully clothed, lying on sofa cushions on the floor, wearing hiking boots, just in case I might have to leave quickly. I spent hours poring over an Army wilderness survival guide, which I had purchased online. This knowledge, although valuable, was perhaps not terribly useful for one living at 103rd and Riverside Drive: not too many edible berries in the median strip.

I hailed a cab right away and made it down the thirty-six blocks to Burt's building and got in the elevator, where I chatted with Ferdo, the nice elevator guy, as we went up.

That all went well, so the next day I decided to tough out this craziness and walked to the Royale bakery a few blocks away. The Royale bakes *kulichi*, the traditional Russian Easter bread. And I needed a *kulich* in order to celebrate Orthodox Easter in the traditional way. So I walked to Seventy-second Street from Sixty-seventh and looked at the ground the whole time, and it went OK. But when I was in the bakery line, the wave of panic came toward me again. I started seeing mental pictures of all the people in New York climbing on top of each other like cockroaches in a storm drain. For a moment, I couldn't remember where I was or what I was doing. I just saw thousands and thousands of people climbing on top of each other, trying to get out of the city.

Something in me knew I had to buy that bread. It knew I had to stay in that line. I concentrated all my mental power on the back zipper of the dress of the woman in front of me. She wore a kelly green linen-blend dress, an old dress on an old woman. I'll never forget its metal zipper tab.

I got the bread. I paid for the bread. I ran to the street and found a cab, and in the five blocks to Burt's apartment I recited everything religious that came to my mind, which, I am sad to say, wasn't all that much. I repeated the Twenty-third Psalm over and over because my mother had taught me the Twenty-third Psalm when I was nine years old, and I tried to remember "The Windhover" but only got as far as daylight's dauphin. As the cab inched through traffic, I could feel my brain shutting down, like one overloaded transformer blowing after another. I thought I was going crazy, I thought I was losing my mind. I decided to count back from a hundred to zero, to make sure that I could. I made it to ninety-four but then blanked on the next number. The cab stopped, and I got up to the apartment and didn't come back out.

Talk about the houseguest from hell. I was terrified all the time, afraid that Burt would leave the apartment, afraid to be alone, afraid that if I left the building I would get lost and never be found again. The next day he took me on a walk around the block. I gripped his hand like a child. I don't remember the doctor or the pills that kept me asleep most of the time. I don't remember Burt's quiet phone calls to my sister in Washington state. I don't remember his taking me to the airport. But when I came out of the plane on the other side of the country, I remember Anna standing inches from the hatch, smiling, blonde hair flowing, strong mother-hand reaching for mine.

When life falls apart, you can do one of two things. You can build a box and hide in it. Or you can walk around in the rubble and learn from it that all boxes eventually crumble. I had spent my life chasing the perfect. I had spent years and years trying to control the pain of living by designing it out of the plan. And when, one by one, the structures that I believed in dissolved, my life collapsed around me like a house of Eames cards. Hiding in a nine-by-sixteen-foot room only made me lose touch with reality. It did not help me overcome panic; it only kept the panic outside four walls. And it kept me from living a real life, a life that mixes friendship and work and pain and love in the big soup pot. When I think of that time, I think of it as a metaphor for the modern-design response. And that's why I have described it to you.

The modernists built us a box—a box of rules and grids and values that keep the pain of reality at bay. That box allows us to intellectualize, to be ironic, to speak of "architectonics" in cool rooms to wealthy students. It allows us to forget the demands of real life. It allows us to believe that we can rise above those demands in pursuit of fulfillment, ignore them in our idealistic and ego-driven search for perfection.

Living inside the box did not make things better for me. Teaching the box has not made things better for design. Teaching ironic distance, a disregarding of reality, a belief in our own narrow, and often narrowly educated, view of the world has not made design better; it has made it an exercise in novelty and in narcissism.

The day after I got to Seattle, my sister found a cognitive psychologist who specialized in panic attacks, and she took me over to see him. Dr. Sholl, like the sandal, only without a "c." He gave me a test. I am a test-taker: I love a test. I was proud to get such a high score, until he explained that high was not good. He said I was depressed, that anxiety is aggravated depression. I told him I was not depressed. He said that I was so depressed that if I wanted to go to the hospital, he would take me there himself.

"Anxiety is aggravated depression." Fear and sadness go hand in hand. I think that's what happened to designers after World War I. The people who survived that war responded to their deep sadness

Pascal Verbena

Holocaust, 1988, detail

with depression or anxiety. And if they were anxious, they reached out to control, without knowing what they were doing. They decorated their little room and told themselves that if they got it right, if they made it perfect, then they would never have to go out of that room, life would cease to be terrifying, and the world would cease to be brutal.

I spent two months at Anna's, doing laundry while wearing sunglasses. Still afraid to be alone, I found separating darks and whites very soothing, though I had some rough moments with decision-making regarding the true meaning of "lights." This may have had something to do with the sunglasses. My nephew Wes, then seven, took me exploring in the wetland near the house, and we whacked a lot of things with cattails. I remember sitting in a huge pile of Bubble Wrap and cardboard eating strawberries with my five-year-old niece, Annie-O. But mostly I slept, and waited for the trees to look normal again, waited for them to stop looking like the work of a desperate gene. Burt had sent the *kulich*, the Easter bread, along with me, packed neatly in my overnight bag. But Anna and I did not eat it. I did not want it: it sat on the counter, growing stale. At twilight one evening I went out and crumbled it up and tossed the pieces in the wetland, knowing the deer would find it.

For the first time in my life, I believed in nothing: not in the primitive chant of Orthodoxy; not in the clean dreams of modernism; not in the comforting structure of semiotics; not in the value of making things, of effort, of trying. Since I was unable to read or to drive (depression can make letters nonsensical and logical thinking impossible), I followed Anna around on her errands. One day we sat together waiting for Annie-O outside her ballet class. A fellow ballet mother leaned over to Anna and asked if she knew anyone who would like to rent a cottage. Anna's eyes lit up. I removed my sunglasses.

And so, a few days later, I moved into a little house—a child's drawing of a house—surrounded by an overgrown garden, backed by alder woods. It is a tiny house, but it is grand compared to a nine-by-sixteen-foot room. It is as far from 103rd Street and the Hudson River as a person can go without swimming in the Pacific. Many berries here.

I bought a pillow-top mattress at Penney's and lived alone in the bee-loud glade, without a pot or pan, without a book or a computer, until the movers brought my stuff to me. In one of the boxes, I found the unwashed mug from my kitchen counter, the mug I put down on my way out the door that blue evening. It still smelled of kava-kava.

After a few months, a writer I know called me. David is a New Yorker to the bone. He reads everything, assimilates everything, everywhere else is not New York—that type of guy. I answered the phone and he asked, "So how're you doing out there with all those dodos in fleeceland?"

His call caught me in one of those moments in which I was lecturing aloud to myself in the living room. For me, lecturing aloud to myself in the living room is a sign of mental health. It is a sign that I am ready to rise and fight again.

I told him that the dodo was a bird made extinct by the idiocy of mankind. It was massacred because its feathers were softer than down, considered perfect for stuffing small pillows. We like to attribute its extinction to its stupidity, but it was no more stupid than any other bird, it was just softer.

I warmed to my subject and went on, saying that fleece is a spun felt created of man-made fibers. "To fleece" is a verb as well as a noun:

it means "to defraud or swindle." Northwesterners are fleece wearers, but this does not mean they have a corner on fleece between the ears. When it comes to being fleeced, who has been more fleeced than those of us who have lain upon our dodo-down pillows and dreamed only the dreams sanctified by our consuming culture?

I began to walk around the living room, gesticulating boldly with my free hand. I informed him that we search in vain for the Golden Fleece of contentment. Calmed by a soothing media, distracted by an object-pumping consumer culture, we live our lives swathed in the cozy fleece of ignorance. Because our society gives us no real help, no myths to live by, we are unable to come to grips with life, with death, with confusion, failure, or pain. We stumble along, stupid, ignorant, on Matthew Arnold's darkling plain, wearing fleece-covered glasses, like so many blind mice, linked in an economic chain from birth to death. We are *all* dodos in fleeceland.

Silence on the other end of the phone. I breathed deeply, triumphant. New York may have whomped me over the head with one too many two-by-fours; I may have had to take refuge in a cottage on an island in Puget Sound; but my verbal punch was coming back. Silently, I congratulated myself and waited for his acerbic response.

But then he said, "I'm sorry—what were you talking about? I missed what you were saying. I'm mesmerized, sitting here watching the blue come off the river."

THE MANDALA

When she was in her early seventies, my mother began volunteering in the textile department of the Asian Art Museum in San Francisco once a week, on Thursdays. She was already slowing down, and had already had one bout with cancer, but she still had her sight and her hand skills, she still stood erect and was beautiful. And so she worked in a back room at the museum, stabilizing old silks and hangings. At first she had to fight her natural instinct to make the things she worked on look fresh and new again. Fresh and new didn't count in this situation. She was just there to perform triage: just there to stop the bleeding, keep the seventeenth-century kimono from going to pieces, keep the rip in the wall hanging from getting any bigger. She was there to keep things from becoming more worn, to reinforce anything that looked as if it was about to go.

She liked the women she worked with in the textile workroom. Perhaps the camaraderie reminded her of those early days in the millinery studio at John-Fredrics. Though, now, instead of a designer watching her every move, she had a curator. In matters of ego and authoritarianism, she found them similar. Every once in a while this curator would raise my mother's hackles. She'd whirl through the workroom, peppering her orders and comments with "coarse" expressions (my mother's term for profanity that refers to procreative or evacuative activities). This woman, prone to wearing leather pants, was very impressed with the wonderful curatorialness of her own slim-hipped self. Not unlike many executives in the cultural world, she considered volunteers to be a species of dumb animal similar to ox or yak—powerful when harnessed, but not of great individual consequence. Nevertheless, my mother liked working in the textile room: she liked stabilizing things. She liked sitting by the nice woman who was a weaver, and she always came back home refreshed and stimulated.

A year or so after my mother started working there, when she had really settled in, the museum began to ready itself for an exhibition entitled *Wisdom and Compassion: The Sacred Art of Tibet*. As part of the celebration, two monks came from the monastery of the Dalai Lama and began to create a six-foot-wide mandala of colored sand and ground gemstones on a low platform directly under the rotunda of the main hall of the museum. For weeks, they bent low over their work, pouring intricate patterns that symbolized a spiritual conception of the cosmos.

Every Thursday, my mother came to the museum early so that she could watch the monks. She stood silently with the other onlookers, mesmerized by the complexity of the pattern, by the monks' slow, methodical artistry, by their control in pouring their minute streams of color. She got to know one of them. They would smile and say a few words to each other in the back hallways when they passed. The work on the mandala progressed, and every Thursday my mother came home and told us how it was going. How the monks had laid down orange and lavender and white that day, how she had watched them do it.

All my life, I watched my mother pour her talent away. She poured it into small designs, into making a girl's wedding dress, into making a tea party for my grandmother the matriarch. I saw her pour her talent into vessels that it could have burst, had she let it. But she controlled it, pouring it in a fine stream—like sand into a mandala. I spent much of my life angry that her huge talent was frittered away.

My mother was at the museum the day before the mandala was to be completed. And, after her usual watching of the process and her usual short conversation with her monk, she settled down to mending in the textile room. But in the late morning, she heard a sudden screeching and confusion coming from the main hall. She and the other volunteers rushed to see what the trouble was.

As she came around the corner, she saw a woman—disheveled, deranged—reeling on the platform, scuffing the sand and screaming something about "Buddhist death squads." The security guards had just tackled her, and together they swayed and thrashed around, as in a dance, destroying the mandala. The volunteers froze, stunned. Both monks stood to the side. The security guards dragged the woman down from the platform, her cries echoing up the rotunda as they pulled her away.

My mother knew this mandala was to have been temporary. The monks had planned to dismantle it after its months of exhibition, to take it apart, to pour the sand into the sea. She knew that. But this was destruction, not dismantling. No one had been able to see the work. No one would enjoy the completed masterpiece. This was creativity arrested: the heat-killed bud of a flower that would never open.

In her shock, she searched for her monk and found him, but then couldn't think of what to say. Should she apologize for what the crazy woman had done? Should she mourn with him about the destruction of his mandala, so near completion? They looked at each other for a long moment. And then the monk bowed to her. The monk bowed to my mother as though there were no one else in that screech-filled rotunda. He bowed as if no running feet were hastening by, no orders being barked and carried out. He seemed to bow from a great distance. She stood there for a long moment, letting his bow sink in, taking his composure inside her. And then she bowed to him.

And so they stood there in the rotunda of the museum, stood silently together as people rushed around them to hear the story from onlookers and to peer at the destroyed mandala.

When she came home that night, she told me this story as though she were speaking into a recorder. She never did that before; she never did it again. When she came to the bowing, she looked at me hard, as if to pin the story to my mind. As if to lock it in my memory for later, when I would need it.

When my mother died, I thought about how her great talent had been lost, about how all her projects had just blown away, like the sand of that mandala. But then I remembered the way she had looked at me when she told me that story. And I knew then for the first time what she had found out then and had tried to tell me: that the importance of design is in the designing moment—that the value of life is in the living moment, and not in what remains behind.

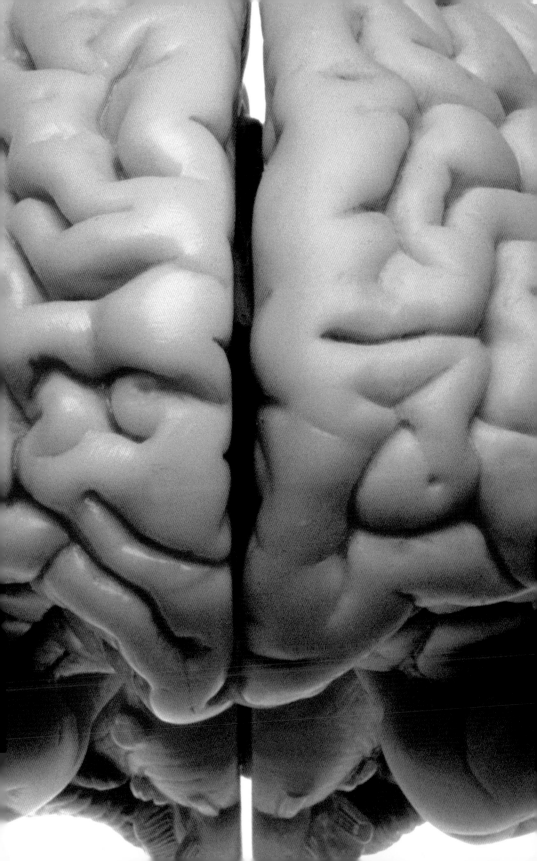

TANYA AND MARINKA

When I was twelve, my father retired from the foreign service, and our family moved from Virginia to California, where I met my twin aunts, Tanya and Marinka, for the first time. They looked exactly alike, such perfect copies of each other that the FBI kept coming back to study them, intrigued by their identical fingerprints. They were in their early sixties but hadn't lost the soft, husky Russian accents that marked them as refugees from the Soviet Union. And though they never tried to dress in the same way, similar choices occurred to both of them, genetically. Each had a long, silver pageboy haircut and sported Miles Davis–style black-rimmed glasses. Each wore slim little black slacks, a black turtleneck, and tiny black high-heeled boots when she appeared at a party. When they appeared together, we were charmed senseless.

Split from the same egg, they had the same genetic constitution. But they were opposites in personality. When she was young, Marinka bore an uncanny resemblance to Carmen, Bizet's wild, operatic young thing. She learned to play the castanets and flounced about with quite a bit of flair. But the young Tanya, so shy that meeting a stranger caused her physical pain, bowed her head and tried to hide her face under her hair, a silent Veronica Lake. Marinka threw things. Tanya refused to dodge. Neither was a wimp. They mellowed in later years, but the differences remained—and intensified.

I grew up in a house of old sofas and tumbling dust balls. My father was always painting a screen or a huge canvas in the family room. My mother always had some large, corded piece of upholstery draped on the sofa, bristling with pins. For such creative people, my parents didn't have a lot of visual sense when it came to the day-to-day, and one could have quite an Oscar Madison–like adventure just trying to find a ringing phone. But when my family went to visit Tanya in her Asian-inspired home for the first time, we trampled in and found ourselves standing upon a large expanse of white rug. An Eames chair stood marooned in the middle distance. Somewhere far off to the left, a white leather banquette registered in the dazzled mind. Not a spot, not a spill, not a variation of shade. Tanya's living room was the white of Plaka, an untracked marvel unaccustomed to the reality of visitors. My sisters and I stood amazed and a bit cowed, each privately wondering about the condition of her soles.

A portrait painter, Tanya also kept her studio in perfect order. Everything stood composed—clean brushes, heavy easel, sitter's chair—like objects in a contemporary Vermeer. Her house itself was a work of art, homage to all things essential and elegant, to all things designed and controlled. It was a refutation of all things illogical, of all things confused and therefore—I must say it—of all things typically Russian. (You'll notice how quickly Constructivism came and went in the USSR. Some say it was a political crackdown. I say it was a bad fit with the Russian mind. Too much white space, not enough murky *lampada* light, not enough mumbling and bowing.)

The two sets of Boratynski twins: Adya and Nicholas, Marinka and Tanya

Tanya was my first modernist, though I did not yet know what a modernist was. The dappled light on her bamboo terrace spoke to me of a heaven where all things were clean and free of dark corners and arranged on a perfect white rectangle. I kept that ordered world in the back of my mind, as a sort of bunker of calm. It was a place to which I could retreat, should the going get too confused.

When our car stopped in front of Marinka's house in Davis, our family plunged in again, this time into a place that looked as though a small incendiary device had gone off right before our arrival. We felt comfortable, for this was what we were used to, and none of us thought it odd to eat around a dinner table with a large sewing machine sitting at one end. Marinka designed costumes and taught costume design. To sit down, you had to move the stack of half-finished velvet doublets that lay on the sofa or redistribute the feather masks piled on the chairs. It was all very warm and creative and including, but it was too much like home for me, and I kept thinking back to Tanya's house, back to that white and that order and that light.

By the time I was a teenager, mine were longer black jeans and lower black boots, but I cultivated Tanya's minimalism, her coolness, her calm. Sadly, all this was not innate, and something broke in my forties.

As the years went by, Tanya slipped into reclusiveness. She would spend hours contemplating a juniper topiary, then, gathering her nerve, make the thought-through cut. She began to avoid other people, preferring the company of her Felco #6 shears, and finally wafted quietly into a nursing home, where she is today. But Marinka continued to mix it up. She listened to the love lives of her students while the pasta water boiled. She listened to the love lives of their professors. She did not comment on overlap. She listened to the political woes of university administrators (the love-life substitute of the career educator), and when she died, they named a building after her.

Yet I followed Tanya. I wanted that streamlined life, that life that admitted no clutter. I went to design school, I memorized the names and the objects and the theories. Later I taught the names and the objects and the theories. And it was only a little while ago that I understood how much I had kept from myself. For me, Tanya and Marinka represent the two halves of human consciousness, the two halves of human existence. Our bodies are dual: two legs, two arms, two feet. Our brains are dual: left brain and right brain. Sex is dual; language is dual, depending as it does on a speaker and a listener. But when I design today, I design in a language and in a mental world that is not dual, but one-sided.

As a student, I sat in the dark and watched the same design-history slides that every other design student watches: the slides that begin with the caves at Lascaux and end with someone like Irma

Boom or Tadao Ando or Mark Kapka, depending on whether it's a lecture on graphic design, architecture, or furniture design. These slides link together the unlinked. They make the design past appear seamless, premeditated, a logical progression out of the caves and into the sunlight. It is as though only Tanya ever lived, as though a celestial plan of progression is borne out in those slides, and that it was only a matter of time, say, until Futurism developed from all that had gone before it. Which is not true. Which is picking up only one thread of a wide weaving.

I learned about design that way, the linear way, and I started to picture myself as the next slide on the carousel. And if you design, you must have, too. In thinking of ourselves this way, we participated not in a conversation but in a monologue—a monologue I listened to and believed in most of my designing life: the one-sided, perfectionistic, patriarchal, life-ignoring monologue of modernism.

Tanya and Marinka were born about the same time that the Bauhaus produced its radical manifesto. Like Martin Luther nailing his ninety-five theses to the church door, the Bauhaus nailed up its tenets of what design should be in 1919, and to this day modernism is our basic design philosophy. Whatever we think or do or say, no matter how carefree we feel with Alias or how nonchalantly we design with form•Z, no matter how apolitical we think we are or how much fun we have, we are reacting to or reevaluating or excavating or denying or following a set of notions that were invented almost a hundred years ago.

Modernism—pre, post, or neo—idealizes the cutting edge, the hot, the cool, the killer. The idea that something is hot means that something else is tepid. The idea that something is killer—well, I

1928

1949

In 1928, Jan Tschichold wrote his extremely influential "The New Typography," a manifesto of modern thought that champions sans serif typefaces and asymmetrical page layouts while rejecting serifed typefaces, symmetry, and centered arrangements.

Tschichold's ideas were to typography and graphic design what Gropius's were to architecture. Unlike Gropius, however, Tschichold later synthesized his pre- and post-manifesto ideas, and returned to including serifed faces, centered type, typographic ornaments, and the occasional line drawing in his work.

suppose the opposite would be life affirming. (God forbid.) The idea of one thing being cooler or hotter than another is the idea that there is a hierarchy in good design, and hierarchy is a mythically male concept. (When I say male, I don't mean manly in the Irish Spring sense. I mean individualistic, intellectual, achieving, as opposed to the mythically female: mystical, chthonic, intuitive, tied to the body. One is about the outer world, the other about the inner.)

Modernism is the great flowering of all that is mythically masculine, sky cult: it has its roots in Enlightenment thinking, in the cult of the individual. It is all that is Apollonian, leaning heavily on the Greek ideal of the "light of the mind," on the notion that the human mind is the apex of creation's achievement. It depends on intellect, on ratios and percentages, on a borrowed classicism, on mathematical formulae. Modernism is aerodynamic, it is ascendant, it is dominant. Modern planes fly above us; modernist buildings soar above us.

When we idealize the top of the hierarchy—one side of the tape measure—we encourage the perfect and discourage the real. Apollonian perfectionism leaves out half of human experience. Its basic intellectual and emotional shortcomings leave us nowhere to be the complex human beings we are. At the same time, and without our particular consent, modernism denies all that is mythically feminine, tribal, clannish, communal, earth walking. We Westerners are a people of the left brain; we make no room for that which is messy, not linear, not essential, uncontrolled.

Even the good old postmodern era, which allegedly championed imperfection, only did so in ways that "perfected" the imperfect, lifting the vernacular from its lowly low to a lofty, if ironic, high. Old motel signs and Las Vegas ducks were the outsider art of modernism. We designers framed the colored-pencil drawing—laboriously done by the schizophrenic in his mother's basement—hung it on the wall of our nice clean museum, and called it art. Postmodernism depended, as did poststructuralism, on the intellect, on irony, on quoting obscure philosophers, mastering the high and the low, the elite and the popular, doctrine and ideology. In the end, the theories of decenteredness and meaninglessness and paradox became paradoxically central and meaningful to academic hierarchies and tenure review boards all over the planet. This could be called ironic.

I must admit one thing. Those aging academics who earned their stripes hiding in doorways during the Paris riots of 1968, who insisted that design be socially conscious and stole with both hands from the word-hoards of cultural and literary criticism, did try to break the stranglehold that the International Style had on us. They tried to show what lay on the other side of the glossy brochure. We must give them that.

Now, though, the lovely liquid buildings of today's young architects are a repackaging of good old modernism. This time there is less verbal posturing involved, because one's hoary professors were poststructuralists and they talked everything into pounded poi. Luckily, all the decisions of modernism have already been coded into the software of the tools. The fulmination is predigested. Your palette may have three million available decisions, but all those three million decisions are predetermined for you by the creator of the program.

These architects see their work in the very way that those good old modernists saw their own work. "Let's take these new industrial tools," they say, "and see what we can make that is essential, and find in that essentialism something perfectly beautiful." No literary hoo-

Asymptote
Proposal for Technology Culture
Museum, New York City
1999
Project commissioned and
supported by *Architectural Record*,
"Millennium" special issue,
Dec. 1999

Janine Antoni

Gnaw, 1992

ha for us. Perfectly beautiful, perfectly essential. Perfectly individual-istic and award-winning. Perfectly suited to causing a ruckus at the Venice Biennale. And missing something big.

Modernism is nothing if not adaptable. A hundred years ago it was hammered into a system that allowed us to ignore the unacademic, irrational, mysterious part of ourselves. Fifty years ago, it provided corporations with the perfect masking tool. Thirty years ago, it gave young academics something to kick against. And even ten years ago, it allowed us to hide our greed with the clean lines of a $10,000 black walnut table. But now it gives *us* a place to hide.

We all watched the second plane hit the World Trade Center tower. We saw the clip over and over, watched that repeated moment of impact: the rising sun's reflection shaking on the windows of the huge building, the tower absorbing the jet whole. Twin jets aimed at twin towers. Identical towers that stood as a symbol of America's economic power—yes, but towers that also stood for the modernist pride of American architecture. They proclaimed our power through their dominance, facelessness, intellect. That collision can be seen as more than the enormous waste of life the terrorists planned. It is a symbol for the repressed power of the ignored—for the primitive revenge that one side of our communal unconscious can exact on the other side's supremacy.

That day, we watched the brutal side of human consciousness strike a horrific blow to the clean, antiseptic, temperature-controlled, and falsely secure side. Witnessing this has made us different. Yet we all know people who, after a few shocked days, turned back to their computer screens and engrossed themselves in designing, say, a nice, liquid building. Design can be so comforting, particularly when people are not involved.

This belief in control, that somehow building the tallest tower or the fastest jet is going to save us from the ugly side of life—from death, really—is the fundamental lie of modernism. And we believe it. We forget about the balance we must find if we are going to be whole people, a whole culture. And that's why modernism has failed us. It denies the fulfillment of the other half of the mind, the other half of experience, the other half of human consciousness. In its thrall, we've taught ourselves not to recognize that person over there, waving at us from the shadows, that person with fingerprints identical to ours—that female part of the designing mind—our Marinka.

Ed Ruscha
The Los Angeles County
Museum on Fire, 1972

ACKNOWLEDGMENTS

This book took its sweet time forming in the maelstrom that is my unconscious mind, and a number of people helped me pull on the thing to finally get it out.

Cullen Stanley, my literary agent at Janklow & Nesbit, has been a mainstay of encouragement. I am honored that she regularly unfurls her considerable gifts for my benefit.

Susan S. Szenasy, editor in chief of *Metropolis* magazine, had the idea for the book and waited for it patiently through months of drafts and recastings.

Martin C. Pedersen, executive editor of *Metropolis* magazine, went a number of rounds on the manuscript, and gave me courage when things looked really black.

When Diana Murphy, the editorial director of Metropolis Books, came to the project, she brought her big lumpy bag of tools along, and the book has benefited from her honing. It could not have been completed without her fine wit, enthusiasm, and thoughtful guidance.

Matthew Monk designed the book and its jacket, suggested the illustrations, and added a depth to the project that would not have been there without him. He has been a true collaborator.

At D.A.P., Adrian Crabbs, Alexander Galán, Cory Reynolds, Avery Lozada, and Sabrina Mansouri have collectively put their shoulders to the grindstone for the book. Which would explain their narrow shoulders. I think I mean noses. Anyway, they have risked body parts for the project, and got the book out in front of you.

I envy Anne Thompson her fine copyeditor's hand.

Conversations with students around the country helped me think many of my ideas through. Christopher Ozubko and Doug Wadden at the University of Washington; Dawn Barrett and Nancy Skolos at the Rhode Island School of Design; and Greg Murphy, Margo Halverson, and Charles Melcher at the Maine College of Art made those conversations possible.

I appreciate so much the support of my family and friends: My sister Anna Ilyin McClain continues to be the first person to read and edit anything I write and is a constant source of real encouragement. My sisters Nadia Ilyin and Alexandra Ilyin cheerlead tirelessly, as do my father, Boris Ilyin, and his wife, Mary. Many a large and silent box of frozen steaks has shown up at my door just because Donna and Dimitri Ilyin worry about my eating right. Annie-O, Wes, and Tanya keep me updated on developments in the real world, and Harris's smile and pudgy knees could inspire a rock. Graham Baran-Mickle kept my spirits up with his daily ring of the doorbell and bright smile on the porch during some pretty rainy days. Janet Livingstone listened to a lot of half-conceived notions and somehow made sense of them so I could move on with the book. Thérèse Caouette understood everything without my having to tell her. Kristin von Kreisler brought hope and enthusiasm along with her elegant self. Flash Rosenberg made me laugh and think, sometimes simultaneously. Mark Petry provided mental clarity when ideas got murky. Richard le Blond kept a fire crackling on the hearth and produced big pots of Lapsang souchong at a moment's notice. Thomas Goryeb has believed in me and supported my writing wholeheartedly over the years, sometimes at real cost to himself. And Peter Spencer put music where darkness had been.

NOTES

1 Voltaire once said, "Those who can make you believe absurdities can make you commit atrocities."

2 Now don't write to me and tell me that you draw like Raphael and have since the third grade. I am talking in gross generalities here.

3 Not all American designers welcomed the Bauhaus refugees with open arms. Frank Lloyd Wright, whose philosophy of an "organic architecture" included considerations of site and inhabitants, hated Gropius's architecture with a passion. When Gropius came to Harvard and placed a formal introductory telephone call to Wright at his studio Taliesin West, Wright summarily hung up on him.

4 This is the only real reason to write. Don't let anyone fool you. Writing is the only way to get thoughts of Self out of your system so you can go out and make a living doing something else.

5 Gropius wasn't the only ex-cavalry officer leading the modernist charge. Alexey Brodovitch saw action as a captain in the Russian cavalry during World War I and was wounded while fighting for the White Army during the Russian Revolution. Neither seems to have let his saber rust.

6 Unfortunately, Pevsner follows up this great statement with "and as long as this is the world and these are its ambitions

and problems, the style of Gropius and other pioneers will be valid," which I don't agree with at all. Nikolaus Pevsner, *Pioneers of the Modern Movement* (London: Faber and Faber, 1936), rev. ed., *Pioneers of Modern Design* (Harmondsworth: Penguin, 1991), 217.

7 Matthew Arnold, "Dover Beach," in M. H. Abrams, gen. ed., *The Norton Anthology of English Literature*, 3rd ed., vol. 2 (New York: W. W. Norton, 1974), 1356.

8 Read Darwin.

9 Ernest Becker, *The Birth and Death of Meaning* (New York: Free Press, 1971), 187. I would quote the whole book had I the room.

10 Ibid., 186.

11 Irrefragable means incapable of being refuted or controverted.

Wilhelm Worringer, *Abstraction and Empathy* (Chicago: Ivan R. Dee, 1997), 24. Worringer's book was first published in 1908 in Germany as *Abstraktion und Einfühlung* and in 1953 in the United States.

12 Traditionally, the "name designer" gets the work and puts his imprimatur on a project, but the actual designing is done by several nameless young people who work for $13,000 a year and live five to an apartment in the East Village.

90, Andy Warhol, *Before and After No. 3*, 1961, acrylic on canvas, 54 x 70 in., private collection, San Francisco, © 2005 Andy Warhol Foundation for the Visual Arts/ Artists Rights Society (ARS), N.Y.; 92, 99, Pascal Verbena, details from *Holocaust*, 1988, mixed media, private collection, photograph by Betsey Wells Farber; 102, "Dodo," engraving, in George Shaw, *Zoological Lectures Delivered at the Royal Institution in the Years 1806 and 1807* (1809), General Research Division, The New York Public Library, Astor, Lenox and Tilden Foundations; 110, photograph by Wernher Krutein, www.photovault.com; 113, 128, courtesy Natalia Ilyin; 118 left, Jan Tschi- chold, *The New Typography: A Handbook for Modern Designers*, trans. Rauri McLean (Berkeley: University of California Press, 1995), xxi; right, Rauri McLean, *Jan Tschichold: A Life in Typography* (New York: Princeton Architectural Press, 1997), 79; 121, courtesy Asymptote; 122, Janine Antoni, *Gnaw*, 1992, chocolate, lard, lipstick, and display case, variable dimensions, courtesy the artist and Luhring Augustine, N.Y.; 124, Ed Ruscha, *The Los Angeles County Museum on Fire*, 1972, oil on canvas, 53 $1/2$ x 133 $1/2$ in., Hirshhorn Museum and Sculpture Garden, Smithsonian Institution, Gift of Joseph H. Hirshhorn, photograph by Lee Stalsworth